Music Therapy and Addictions

of related interest

Early Childhood Music Therapy and Autism Spectrum Disorders
Developing Potential in Young Children and their Families
Edited by Petra Kern and Marcia Humpal
Foreword by David Aldridge
ISBN 978 1 84905 241 2
eISBN 978 0 85700 485 7

Forensic Music Therapy
A Treatment for Men and Women in Secure Hospital Settings
Edited by Stella Compton Dickinson, Helen Odell-Miller and John Adlam
Foreword by Estela V. Welldon
ISBN 978 1 84905 252 8
eISBN 978 0 85700 539 7

Voicework in Music Therapy
Research and Practice
Edited by Felicity Baker and Sylka Uhlig
Foreword by Diane Austin
ISBN 978 1 84905 165 1
eISBN 978 0 85700 480 2

Music and Altered States
Consciousness, Transcendence, Therapy and Addictions
Edited by David Aldridge and Jörg Fachner
ISBN 978 1 84310 373 8
eISBN 978 1 84642 464 9

The Music Effect
Music Physiology and Clinical Applications
Daniel J. Schneck and Dorita S. Berger
Illustrated by Geoffrey Rowland
ISBN 978 1 84310 771 2
eISBN 978 1 84642 462 5

Adolescents, Music and Music Therapy
Methods and Techniques for Clinicians, Educators and Students
Katrina McFerran
Foreword by Tony Wigram
ISBN 978 1 84905 019 7
eISBN 978 0 85700 376 8

Suicide
The Tragedy of Hopelessness
David Aldridge
ISBN 978 1 85302 444 3
eISBN 978 0 85700 081 1

A Non-Violent Resistance Approach with Children in Distress
A Guide for Parents and Professionals
Carmelite Avraham-Krehwinkel and David Aldridge
ISBN 978 1 84310 484 1
eISBN 978 0 85700 217 4

Music Therapy and Addictions

Edited by David Aldridge and Jörg Fachner

Jessica Kingsley *Publishers*
London and Philadelphia

First published in 2010
by Jessica Kingsley Publishers
116 Pentonville Road
London N1 9JB, UK
and
400 Market Street, Suite 400
Philadelphia, PA 19106, USA

www.jkp.com

Copyright © Jessica Kingsley Publishers 2010
Printed digitally since 2012

Library of Congress Cataloging in Publication Data
A CIP catalog record for this book is available from the Library of Congress

British Library Cataloguing in Publication Data
A CIP catalogue record for this book is available from the British Library

ISBN 978 1 84905 012 8
eISBN 978 0 85700 294 5

Contents

Introduction: Coherence and Timing

David Aldridge

Welcome to this book on music therapy and addictions. As you will see from the table of contents, there are many substances and activities to which we can become addicted. I say we, because one of the difficulties inherent in being a therapist, or indeed a writer about the problems of being human, is that we take a stance of 'we' the healthy, and the sick as 'other'. This has been perhaps colourfully expressed in terms of sociological research as a propensity for researching 'nuts, sluts and perverts'. Indeed, those who take a walk on the wild side of life may appear attractive to the neophyte researcher in the social sciences. For those who have walked on the wild side, and may sometimes still wander across the tracks, the borders between deviance and normality become blurred, as do conventional classifications of sick and healthy behaviour. As many of us know, the basis of our research quest may itself be to conquer what we most fear, or to involve ourselves vicariously in what we find forbidden but attractive.

This book then is a plea for an acceptance of those whom we see as the 'other'. And as such it can be seen to be understood as the imperative of tolerance, which is, of course, a personal plea.

As soon as we begin to use substances for pleasure, or for reasons that challenge normal behaviour, then we are in danger of being classified as deviant: as substance abusers, addicts, junkies, drinkers. There is a continuing nurture versus nature debate about the causes of such challenging behaviour. This debate can be condensed to the questions 'Are we born deviant?' or 'Are we made deviant by those around us?' In some way this is a Shakespearean perspective. As Malvolio says in *Twelfth Night*, 'Some are born great, some achieve greatness and others have greatness thrust upon them.'[1] Maybe we

---

1   Shakespeare, W. *Twelfth Night*. II. vi. 159, Olivia's Garden.

could substitute the word deviance for greatness in the previous sentence: 'Some are born deviant, some achieve deviance and others have deviance thrust upon them'.

The perspective that I will be taking in this chapter is Batesonian. I urge anyone working in this area to read Gregory Bateson's (1973) chapter 'The Cybernetics of Self: A Theory of Alcoholism' in his *Steps to an Ecology of Mind*.[2] He reminds us that the alcoholic is an example of the modern split between mind and body where an attempt is made to escape from our own insane premises that are continually supported by the surrounding society. The basis of alcoholic behaviours is a reflection of the same thinking that leads us to see man versus environment, nation versus nation, chosen religion against religion, God versus man. This thinking emphasises power and control, rather than seeing ourselves as part of an ecology that needs complementarity and cooperation, the basis of which is acceptance. Bateson sees the solution of the problem of a completely different kind. The problem is spiritual. In other words, in our addictions we seek to satisfy our own needs but at the wrong level, the physical rather than the emotional or existential. Indeed, the process of satisfaction demands more of the same unsatisfying material substance, which can become physiological addiction, although the need to be satisfied is non-material. Bjerg (2008) argues that, in a capitalist society, the goal of desire is not to satisfy itself but to repeat itself. Enjoyment, when it is mediated by sensual perception, is part of a social system of regulation. The problem with substances is that they restrict us solely to the body. There is no transcendence. The desire for anything else is eliminated. We repeat our desire(s) without satisfaction.

Becoming deviant does not arise through the deliberate, knowing choice of the actor and it is essentially beyond his or her own control. In such a way, when children behave badly, it is not necessarily their fault, nor that of their parents. It is simply a way of trying to regulate relationships within the family and with the outside world. What I call the ecology of family life is out of balance. We do not have to blame the deviant child, nor inadequate parents. Strangely enough, it is just this issue of control that we bring to the fore regarding people who are addicted and to whom we ascribe an axis of responsibility that locates the problem solely in them. Not only that, the problem for the addicted person is also that we need to prove, and always erroneously, that we are in control.

---

2   My thanks to Vibeke Steffen, University of Copenhagen, for returning me to this chapter, and her insights into the problems of alcoholism from an anthropological perspective.

I am not trying to avoid personal responsibility here. Like every other drinker, I know it is me that picks up the glass. However, when my drinking is seen as deviant, it is not simply a social process, but located within a social network.

Construing behaviour as deviant is a social and political process and the failure to obey group rules. However, it is an ambiguous state, as a person may belong to different groups with different rules. The same behaviour may be construed differently in different cultures and at different times; one cultural rebel may be another culture's innovator. This relativistic view emphasises that the deviance is not the quality of the act, but a consequence of the act. Deviance becomes a political process involving the responses of other people to the behaviour. The meaning of behaviour as being disruptive, and therefore challenging, is a political process of interpretation that must be negotiated after the act. This process is also at the core of all therapeutic encounters.

Deviance is required in social systems because it serves several important positive functions. Such behaviour is induced, if not arising spontaneously, sustained and regulated within a social context. It makes sense then, in attempting to change behaviour through therapy, if we understand such deviance in a sociocultural context.

The presence of deviant behaviour and accompanying sanctions serves an important purpose of defining normative boundaries. Deviant behaviour exemplifies the kinds of action that are not allowed, and sanctions show what will happen if such acts occur. Deviant acts and their accompanying sanctions provide concrete models for social rules. This is always apparent from the way in which we talk about drinking behaviour in social situations regarding juvenile behaviour, driving and potential damage to health.

Every family group will define what constitutes deviance in its own way, for example not working, drinking too much, eating too little, being inappropriately sad, being noisy, being incontinent, sleeping a lot, not sleeping enough, wearing strange clothes, talking nonsense, not concentrating, not listening, answering back or working too hard. This depends upon an actively maintained set of rules and is a social construing which each of us knows. In this way we are informed by and inform such a construing: both personal and social construings are interactive. Any behaviour may serve as evidence of deviance to maintain social viability.

The presence of a deviant person satisfies a certain need for predictability; by labelling one person 'deviant', we are allowed to occupy the status of normality by contrasting them with the 'others'. We need our deviants to keep us on the straight and narrow.

Deviant behaviour is a normal function in social systems which introduce necessary change to maintain stability (Aldridge 1998). What is defined as deviant is based upon the context in which the behaviour occurs and, like any other extreme form of behaviour, this phenomenon is embedded in a wide social, cultural and political context of place and time. Drinking, for example, is an accepted social activity with a complex set of cultural rules that vary according to local cultures. Indeed, most of my best stories are about escapades involving alcohol and friends.

I started drinking beer at the age of ten, accompanied by a cigarette (the wild and wonderful Wills Woodbine), as an introductory process of becoming a man in a working class man's world. If I was going to go into the pub, I had to learn to drink, smoke and play dominoes. By the age of 15, I was drinking beer regularly and a regular smoker funded by my part-time job delivering newspapers and working in the supermarket stocking shelves. My friends did the same. We would escape the youth club in the break and sneak into the back room of the pub. By the age of 18, to be a member of a particular group of friends, it was expected that we could drink 12 pints of beer in an evening, not show the effects, and then go dancing until midnight (our so-called 'Twelve O'Clock Club'). With other friends it was the rhythm and blues club on a Saturday night, where it was cool to drink either rum or whisky. By the time I was in university, it was the mid-Sixties, and we were identified by our recreational pursuits. If like me you both played rugby football and hung out with the arts crowd, then the palette of possible substances to use or abuse was rich and varied.

One of my major problems with drugs was not being able to tolerate marihuana, which you can imagine is a real drag if you belong to an arts crowd set at the height of hippydom in the UK during the Sixties. This was further exacerbated by a deep affiliation to the writing of Jack Kerouac, but fortunately he was also a drinker. To my great good fortune, I also belonged to a group of people really active in the folk music scene and that was liberally fuelled with alcohol, predominantly beer.

Jack Kerouac and the Beat Generation had a profound influence on my creative life. It was through them that I was introduced to a whole new range of poetry and music, and to Zen. But more than this, Kerouac offered a dangerously romanticised view of life, which the reader may already discern in my attitude towards alcohol, and even more than this, an awareness of how creating art changes consciousness. Like many others before me, and for Jack Kerouac in particular, the trap was that the substances which change consciousness are unimaginably pleasurable. In the end, it was the abuse of alcohol that was to bring about his death through an abdominal haemorrhage at the age of 47 years.

In *Big Sur*, we read an account of Jack Kerouac's drinking binge that brings him to the very boundaries of his sanity. Indeed the main body of the book is a narrative account of his breakdown. Escaping from his drinking friends on skid row, he moves into the country surrounding Big Sur, California. Yet, once alone he craves the company of friends. Returning to his friends, he brings himself back into the milieu of his drinking. And once he begins to drink, there is no stopping him.

The importance of Kerouac's book is that it reflects, as many of us drinkers know, his awareness of his own weakness and folly. He begins the book groaning after a drinking bout and getting 'silly drunk', although really he had wanted to go into the woods, draw water, chop wood, read and sleep, echoing the classic Zen accounts of everyday reality. He disgusts himself, feels sick, and knows his hopelessness is physical, and spiritual. This hopelessness is brought into contrast by what he refers to as his hopeful rucksack necessary to live in the woods, and it is the rucksack that he picks up to escape his misery.

He then spends three weeks alone in the woods comparing himself to a bhikku contemplative, although he had planned to stay for six weeks. The term 'bhikku' here refers to a Buddhist monk or nun marked primarily by his or her practice of poverty and non-attachment to the material world, who has left their family and worldly pursuits to meditate, living in a forest retreat near a village or town. It is a theme Kerouac has used in his other novels. However, what Kerouac leaves out of his role is that, in exchange for food, the monk or nun had a responsibility to the local community teaching them the ways of religious righteousness. It is this connection of service to a community that balances the solely personal needs. Perhaps typical of much of this Beat movement, practices were taken piecemeal from spiritual disciplines for personal gain and lost the communal perspective, thereby becoming isolated from a broader context. Ironically, it is this connection of service to the local community that would have saved Jack Kerouac from his increasing isolation, itself a feature of escalating distress (see Chapter 9).

Soon Jack Kerouac, becoming fearful of the ocean that he hears beyond the woods, with an impending sense of doom and increasing hopelessness, becomes bored and decides to return to the city. In this case, the city is San Francisco, from where he had escaped three weeks before, and back to his drinking buddies. He himself admits forgetting the horrors and remembers the good times.

Once in San Francisco he learns that his cat has died and he links this to the death of his brother Gerard. This triggers the helplessness he has felt in the cabin and by the seashore. Although his friend warns him not to get into a drinking binge, Jack decides to stay in San Francisco for the excitement and what he refers to as 'that funny little smile of joy' when he drinks. And so he meets with his old friends and feels that anticipatory joy of drinking with friends in the city.

When he is alone, he feels anguish and hopelessness and has to escape to the city. Back in the city, with his friends, he manages his distress through drinking and camaraderie. His writing perspective moves from that of describing himself. He begins to talk of 'we'. It is a ritual where he meets the same friends, up for an adventure. He stays at the same places, uses the same drinks store. His friends are pleased to see him and they remember the good times. He repeats the same drinking adventures. This is a classic cycle of drinking as a means to manage escalating distress. In the face of escalating distress, he self-medicates with alcohol and marihuana. As a strategy of distress management, it has worked for him before. However, the difficulty is that is his only strategy, and the consequences of such a strategy are an increasing threat to his mental stability. Although admitting to an intolerance of marihuana, he continues to smoke, and experiences his own paranoid reaction. What we have to remember here is that, for centuries, self-medication was the only form of distress management (Hirschman 1995; Johnson 1999) and that we live in a society where drug use is accepted to moderate emotions, manage pain and alleviate suffering (Gray 2004).

Eventually, Jack wakes again, as he did at the start of the book, having passed out drunk the night before, with a headache and groaning, longing for the cabin in the woods. He knows he is caught in a trap of his own making.

This is perhaps a typical cycle of oscillation between the two extremes that we find in drinkers' stories. He escapes the social drinking milieu that is so dangerous for him, but then, faced with himself, he becomes hopeless and bored. To relieve this boredom and distress, he returns to the drinking milieu. While the drinking is a temporary respite, it too brings another form of desperate hopelessness.

Some perspectives on drinking

Well, the best place for a perspective on drinking is obviously a bar but, failing that, sociologists and other such reprobates have kept themselves out of drinking dens by musing on the nature of addiction. We all have our own ways of coping.

A problem of addiction is that we become caught up in a world that is temporally restricted. Condemned to repeating the same cycles of behaviour, as we see in Jack Kerouac, the future becomes increasingly questionable as it collapses into an extended present. It becomes difficult for the self to move forward and develop. We define ourselves by a dynamic projection into the future. This projection of what we will become breaks down if we become chronically sick, mentally ill or addicted. In a society where great emphasis is placed upon being a self-determining individual, then our very identities are threatened. If we are expected to confront the world alone through self-realisation then we are faced with an increasing insecurity, particularly when traditional social forms, such as the family and work groupings, are becoming increasingly fluid or tenuous. For Jack Kerouac, we also see how the group of friends he relied upon to maintain his identity actually maintained with him an identity of the 'drinker', albeit the rebellious artist, effectively locking him in time as repeated cycles of drinking. His personal strategy of distress management fitted his social ecology. Although individual friends tried to counsel him away from drink, he always had enough drinking buddies and hangers-on to keep him company. His immediate future becomes stable, but stabilises into a pattern of drinking that threatens his health and eventually restricts his creative output. When his strategy of distress management promotes more suffering, then we see a long-term pattern of escalating distress (Aldridge 1998; see also Chapter 9). More of the same attempted problem resolution – drinking – only exacerbates the problem and eventually kills him.

Besides this temporal restriction, we are also subjected to a corporeal restriction. Craving works at a bodily level (Bjerg 2008), and our bodies have a social reality that is non-symbolic. It is this viscerality that is so often ignored as it is a form of consciousness not immediately available to interpretation (Weinberg 2002). As Bateson (1973) writes, the self is effectively divided against itself as body and mind. However, meanings become embodied in social activities that are not available immediately to reflection. They are simply performed spontaneously in the moment. Much of our social lives are prior to conscious interpretations. Most of my drinking narratives, like those of Jack Kerouac, are social encounters informed by a cultural milieu either of being a young male in a working-class town, or a sporting environment, or with other musicians. Enjoying drinking was not a solitary activity but one of maintaining an identity with peers, part of which was being able to 'drink'. Being a successful accomplished drinker was an element of a positive male identity (as long as the drinker did not appear intoxicated).

Sex, drugs and rock and roll

The self-medication argument is a strong one but many of us drink, smoke and generally deviate out of sheer enjoyment. While Kerouac, as he himself confesses, belonged to the Beat Generation, many of us have a much more Dionysian perspective on using substances. While Kerouac's beat perspective might fit his would-be Zen perspective of poverty ('beat' in this sense meaning tired or beaten down), his writing also describes many situations where he and his other artist friends are clearly hedonists enjoying an alternative lifestyle. 'Beat' in this sense is not despair but belonging to another rhythm and tempo of life.

Kerouac used the term Beat Generation in the late 1940s to refer to being *beat*ific, or blessed, as part of the natural world, although this was short-lived in the woods of Big Sur, and in the restorative powers of jazz and poetry. The Beat writers called for a renunciation of material goods in favour of a rediscovery of the erotic, artistic and spiritual through the use of drink, drugs, sex, music, and the mysticism of Zen Buddhism. And that was the credo that my generation took on board.

This Beat Generation is often linked to the jazz music of the time, jazz being a rebellion against the dominant norms where the jazz musician is a romantic outsider challenging the moral order. Indeed, to be a rebel also meant an aspect of alienation. Bebop musicians referred to 'square' society as the people that conformed to a bourgeois culture. This expectation was extended to my generation when we were young that extended into the hippy generation, just as the punks were to take this alienation one step further. Deviance is a necessary form of social change, but to become deviant we have to have appropriate social forms and there are symbolic codes for the expression of deviance (Lopes 2005). The beatnik, hippy, punk were such social forms and bound up with a concept of 'style', as we will see later.

Which behaviour is deemed to be deviant, or normal, depends upon where we place it on an axis of legitimacy, and that is a cultural decision (Aldridge 1984, 1998). A ten-year-old drinking beer in a pub, as I did, would be taboo in modern Britain. In my community of origin, it was part of growing up. Drinking with my friends, as a teenager, was a completely normal activity on a Saturday night. In modern terms it would be seen as 'binge drinking'. Drinking beer with my folk musician friends was all part of the evening's entertainment (being teetotal would have been seen as wilfully deviant).

Drugs are part of the economy associated with the music scene and are cultural artefacts associated with pleasure and normalised in that context (Sanders 2005). What we partake of, what we wear, what we listen to, how we dance, how we walk and talk are all part of a general 'style'. Just as being 'Beat' had its style, its language, associated music and substances, then every generation since has adopted its own style(s). There are rituals associated with having a good time and these are a normal part of leisure. This normalisation only emphasises how the axis of legitimacy is movable and accommodates the illicit.

Popular music has often been seen as a threat to public order, whether it is jazz in the 1930s, rock and roll in the 1950s, psychedelic music in the 1970s or hip hop in the 1980s. This threat relates to a political shift away from locating deviance in the individual and offers a voice to disenfranchised groups. The alienated are offered an alternative consciousness as a legitimate style that becomes a strength. We see in the way that hip hop shaped African American identity (Trapp 2005) and the way in which music is linked to the expression of attitude that it is not simply personal style but also a cultural awareness. Music offers us an identity (Aldridge 1989; Ruud 1997) and that identity is expressed as 'style'– a way of being.

Rock music is an essential resource in modern life for feeling, being and doing (DeNora 2000). Not only does it offer a resource for meaning, it also offers a style resource for maintaining the coherence of our own narratives. Most of my drinking stories are linked to music settings, either playing with other musicians or in clubs and pubs where music was played. Listening to Chris Farlowe and the Thunderbirds singing 'Out of Time' on the juke box in the Rose Inn on a Saturday night is still alive in my memory, even on those days now when I cannot remember my mobile phone number. As a community worker, much of my time was spent in dark places where drugs were sold and used. I still remember the music I heard then and the repeated thrill of the first four bars of the Byrds playing 'Mr Tambourine Man'.

This self has an identity that is performed in everyday life. Our memories are also part of that performance. We regain the coherence of our lives and self-identity through the way in which we perform our lives now and with others. But what happens if we transgress and perform differently? From being a social drinker amongst friends, we can easily become labelled as an alcoholic and isolated. The axis of legitimacy, in being movable, can also put us into the situation where we are no longer tolerably deviant but pathological. The maintenance of our identity, and the coherence of the self, is a performance in time.

Many substances used for pleasurable activities, alcohol included, can change our sense of time. The danger lies in that when we lose this sense of timing – time being an *activity*, not a property (Aldridge and Aldridge 2008) – then we lose our sense of coherence and our connection with significant others (Aldridge 1998). Junk time, drug time, booze time are episodes that take us out of the coherence of our life narrative lived with others and threatens to leave us isolated (Reith 1999). This is when addiction is debilitating. We lose the time of others and become locked into a time that isolates us from our own narrative coherence. It makes sense then to use a medium based on performance in time, making music, to bring us back into the community of other souls with which we live our lives. The following chapters in this book will demonstrate just how music is being used in this way.

At the beginning of this chapter, I referred to a need that calls to be satisfied. It is non-material and no substance can meet this need. Using substances, while altering consciousness, threatens to take us out of the timing we need to satisfy our coherence as human beings. To maintain a coherent self, we must perform our identities in time, which I argue demands a praxis aesthetic of living performance. We are the jazz, we are the funk.

So why music therapy? For the simple reason that music offers a non-symbolic immediate contact with reality. If the body has its own consciousness not always immediately available to interpretation, we can say the same of music. Music is direct and it is the bridge to other consciousnesses. Consciousness is literally 'knowing with'. Performing music with another person is a way of achieving a vital connection at a fundamental level that is not necessarily conscious at a cognitive level, but at a bodily level. This visceral contact with reality through music is in the same mode as drugs or alcohol – direct and immediate. However, the benefit of performing music is that it is also both integrative and expressive, bringing modes of consciousness together through coherence and timing. We become entrained to others by attachment and through emotional expression. Performing music, like performing ourselves, is not only integrative for personal coherence, but also joins us to others. We are able to express ourselves with a style that is our own but is also informed by and relevant to our culture. Indeed, we perform that culture and therefore, instead of being deviant, we can be heard and seen as creative performers of new realities. We become coherent within and without our selves. The essential element of that coherence, biologically and culturally, is timing.

CHAPTER 1

Music Therapy, Drugs and State-dependent Recall

Jörg Fachner

Using and misusing drugs is an old phenomenon and seems to be one of the anthropological constants of mankind, like eating, drinking, sex and war. It has always been a social problem that the misuse of drugs influences some people more than others. Every decade of debating drugs has produced differing strategies of how and why to treat those that are addicted (Szasz 2003). Brain research in recent years has identified some physiological mechanisms explaining that, once a substance has left a trace in memory, striving for repetition may initiate processes where some individuals lose control completely while others don't. But, as we can read in Erkkilä and Eerola's chapter later in this book, it seems that it is not the substance itself that induces addiction patterns. Addiction can also be seen in gambling. Gamblers develop the same pattern of behaviour as drug addicts (an intense desire to satisfy a need, a loss of control, periods of abstinence and tolerance, increased thinking about the drug or behaviour, continued abuse despite social and occupational problems) (see Yacubian and Büchel 2009, p.348). Longitudinal research has started to observe what it is in a lifetime that makes some people change their life course into addiction, while others are able to use drugs in a controlled manner (Jungaberle *et al.* 2008; Parker, Williams and Aldridge 2002).

Music therapists and educationalists working with maladjusted youth and adolescents with behavioural problems observe how important popular music culture, its lifestyle and identity templates are for their clients (Doak 2003; Forsyth, Barnard and McKeganey 1997; Horesh 2006b; Mark 1986). Music therapists can use elements of popular music to work on rigid and inflexible behavioural patterns in a group setting. This helps the individual to broaden emotional expression and to locate his or her place in the group. Such work is presented by Dijkstra and Hakvoort in this book. Elements of music, like drumming in a shamanic drum circle and inducing a change of consciousness state when repeating and focusing on drumming, might also be used as a substitute for drugs. Winkelman (2003) described the use of such techniques to change the focus of attention away from drug use to a more natural induced altering of consciousness. Music therapists working in prisons are confronted with clients using drugs in and outside of jail or that were put into jail because they broke the laws by dealing drugs (Romanowski 2007; Zeuch 2001). Others working in psychiatric settings are confronted with clients who have used drugs and alcohol to cope with psychic stress, anxiety or depressed mood (Silverman 2003), or they have run into problems while misusing drugs and are facing a drug-induced psychosis (Ross *et al.* 2008).

Later in this book Hedigan, Horesh and Abdollahnejad write about work in therapeutic communities in which integration into group processes is an important feature of the therapeutic process. The tension of being an individual and at the same time being part of a group and how to maintain identity is a step in becoming an adult that is not easily solved. Accordingly, most music therapy work is group work although different strategies and techniques are used (Silverman 2003; 2009). Working with songs is an important tool, as we can read from Abdollahnejad and Ficken later in this book. This technique with substance abusers has also been presented in Baker, Gleadhill and Dingle (2007). Songs may represent stations in the biography of the client and are loaded with episodic memories that they activate in their imagery. Songs can also describe a certain emotional state that is more concretely expressed in the combination of music and words (Howard 1997; Mark 1988).

One problem that music therapists face when using music or songs with addicted clients is that some music might resemble drug memories, and this can be a crucial point in treatment. Especially if the music, that was part of the setting when using drugs, is a cue for using drugs. Those who try to stay abstinent might be haunted by a strong wish to use drugs when listening to those songs. Sounds, rhythms in songs or improvisations in therapy may have some indexical cue for them (Doak 2003; Horesh 2006a; Soshensky 2001). But to think that music here is nothing more than a secondary, conditioned stimulus of former drug use experiences, as behaviourists might start to explain it, seems limited in its perspective.

In this chapter, I will outline some dimensions that take into account what it is that makes the connection of music and drugs so strong and that it cannot easily be substituted by offering music as a more natural way to reward. Cultural anthropology has shown that music and drugs fit well together. This is what we witness when looking into contemporary popular culture and a use of drugs that is embedded in it (see Aldridge in the previous chapter and Manning 2007). When we have situated the use and misuse of drugs in a cultural frame of reference, we discuss the influence of the brain's endogenous reward system and its interaction with music in a context of therapy.

Drugs, music and cultural practice

Social pharmacology is a discipline of pharmacology that focuses on the usage of drugs as consumption behaviour. These behaviours are observed and described in their social environments and are interpreted with pharmacological, sociological and psychological methods. The aim of this approach is to understand or describe patterns of use and resulting risk behaviour (Battisti *et al.* 2006; Gahlinger 2004; Gerhard 2001; Nencini 2002). This data may lead to adjusted prevention and harm reduction strategies, mental health proposals, drug policy or even a modification of corresponding laws. A social pharmacology of music might help us to understand the use of drugs in certain contexts of music activity (Fachner 2004b).

Witnessing the traces of illicit drug use in film, television and print media and listening, reading and watching the references to drug use in the lyrics of popular music, in its sound design, in speech and in the performance and choreography of music videos, one could almost believe drug use has become a normal activity within everyday life of Western civilisation. Manning (2007) looks into normality of popular culture, and what role the media and pop music play for the normalisation of drug use. His central thesis in short is – drug use has a history in Western civilisation, has developed as a cultural practice in its context, and utilises contextualised symbolic frames of reference that identify, represent and rationalise drug use and its functionality within culture.

In the overall debate on the origins of music, Walter Freeman (2000) explored ways in which music and dance were related to the cultural evolution of human behaviour and forms of social bonding. He perceives connections in the traded knowledge on altered states of consciousness caused by chemical and behavioural forms of induction. Trance states produced in this manner served to break through habits and beliefs about reality, but also to make individuals alert for new and more complex information. In times of primarily oral information transfer, memorising techniques were required that stimulated all the senses for storing and processing that information. Musical abilities in particular seemed to be important for an effective transfer of knowledge.

Drugs were discovered in nature and cultivated, used by experienced shamans in initiation rites or for tribal festivities (Metzner 1992), could be found by the wayside, invited to rest or contemplation in kairological moments, caused thoughts to wander or dive into inner worlds, posed the first questions about the nature of reality – as postulated by the ethnobotanist Terence McKenna (1992) – and helped the brain to mature or created a real awareness of a hunger for answers. There were always situations that 'told' intoxicated individuals something and marked an altered state of consciousness (Glicksohn 1993; Rätsch 1992). Whether this happens in dance, in love making or in contemplation depends on individual lifestyle and preferences (Taeger 1988). The ritual of drugs (Szasz 2003) has often created mood, led to states of ecstasy, produced a first-evidence experience (Laing 1967) or gone beyond this world to make contact with new worlds of imagination (Masters and Houston 1968), ideas, visions or even spirits (Rätsch 1992). The combination of music and drugs as a phenomenon specific to the 1960s is certainly not something new. The medieval Austrian poet and singer Walther von der Vogelweide described drunken festivities with wine, women and song at castles in the Middle Ages (Nolte 1991), and the Ancient Greeks even added psychedelic substances (ergot) to the wine for their bacchanalia (Rätsch 1995; Wasson, Hofmann and Ruck 1978).

In a longitudinal study, Howard Parker et al. (2002) have shown that a normalisation of illicit recreational drug use as a leisure activity has become an accepted social reality. Drugs would have become accommodated because of their widespread use in the popular music culture. Using cannabis or MDMA (ecstasy) is not a phenomenon of formerly pathologised and stigmatised subcultures any more, but an accepted and integrated part of youth culture in Western civilisation. Popular culture and music have played an important role in the process of normalisation of recreational drug use as a leisure activity. The use of cannabis or MDMA created a context of meaning of drug use embedded in a historically grown and symbolically mediated frame of reference and corresponding practice within popular culture.

Research on popular music stressed the semiotics of signs used in an artistic context, which produce meanings for performer and audience. Thus, music becomes a mediator of cultural symbols (Tagg 1987). Therefore, several issues of identity, place and performance, musical practice and production styles, mediating experience of a certain song or classic composition in a specific listening, or even music production, situation, are taken into account to understand the aesthetic experience (Kärki, Leydon and Terho 2002).

The pop-cultural mediated identity scheme of 'being different as the others', and its symbolic, and by the same token sensual, representation of the drug-induced 'other' feeling, sensing and perceiving of social reality, has originated its historical equivalents and prototypes in the lifestyles of stars like Louis Armstrong, Charlie Parker, Miles Davis, Jimi Hendrix, Curt Cobain, Amy Winehouse and so on (Fachner 2004a). From the Harlem tea pads of the 1930s to the 1960s rock festivals and chill-out parties of the 1990s rave scene, lifestyle, identity and cultural practice is associated with drug use and corresponding popular artists struggling with their life as outsiders (Becker 1963). 'As a repeated trope, however, the Faustian musical myth revolves around the use of illegal narcotics, allegorises Blake (2007, p.106), the fragile composition of a popular musician's identity being between an inspired hedonistic artist and becoming addicted for the sake of 'being hip' and not 'square'. All the musicians referred to above are linked by their romantic fondness for the Faustian element of their artistic techniques of ecstasy, and the human, all too-human fallibleness as a magician's apprentice: the here and there unsuccessful control of the drug ghosts for their art. Or as Eric Clapton described it:

> To begin with, drink is very baffling and cunning. It's got a personality of its own. Part of the trap [of drugs and alcohol] is that they open the doors to unreleased channels or rooms you hadn't explored before or allowed to be open. A lot of my creative things came out first of all through marijuana. I started smoking when I was about eighteen or nineteen, and that would let out a whole string of humorous things as well as music. Then drink allowed me to be very self-piteous and opened up that whole kind of sorrowful musical side of myself. Unfortunately after that, the booze becomes more important than the doors it's opening, so that's the trap. (Eric Clapton in Boyd 1992, p.199)

Pharmacological determinism

While medical researchers and pharmacologists stress the more or less objective somatic action profile of drugs on our senses and central nervous system functions, in the context of cultural studies on drug use these approaches have been criticised as being much too deterministic and narrowed in their scope on drugs (Manning 2007). When discussing drug use within a symbolic frame of reference, as a cultural practice, as an identity template, as a means for artistic inspiration, then the drug action profile is not the only important matter, but rather what people expect, do, think and experience in situations using the drugs for artistic, ritualistic or hedonistic purposes. Here, the drug effects have been domesticated – as Eichel and Troiden (1978) described it for marihuana – for a certain social or personal intention, in order to party, to get into altered states of consciousness, to be cool, to be hip, bad, far out or different from the others. This is not that the effects are neglected, but being used in an aesthetic context they do not necessarily need to function only in a rational pharmacologically deterministic manner. A classic example is Andrew Weil's (1998) concept of 'inverse tolerance', the observation that the marihuana action profile can be controlled or even be turned off at will from an experienced user. In the early 1970s, this led to many polemical debates between those who, from an anthropological perspective, accepted that an experienced user (as, for example, a shaman) could control the action profile of a known drug for certain purposes and between those who, natural-science based and orthodox deterministic, were not convinced that pharmacological substances and their action profile could be controlled at will.

Social determinism

Becker (1963), in his classic sociological deviance study of marihuana use among jazz musicians, was able to show that recognising and enjoying the effects has to be learned. This is in concordance with anthropologists and their differing descriptions of drug effects of the same pharmacological origin (Blätter 1990). Drugs have been found to produce many different culture-related effects. Becker stressed the cultural context determination of human behaviour even when being under the influence. He questioned the epistemological dimension of pharmacological behaviour determination from his sociological stance as a matter of socially constructed definitions set by groups that have the power to define what is to be perceived under the influence. So, if the frame of reference is set by a peer group of musicians, they may focus on perceiving the well-known cannabis effects on time perception as neat for improvisation and rhythmic variation, while for a group of physicians, the possible dangers of the accelerated heart rate may become a focus of attention.

However, drugs have a certain action profile on the body and this is what makes some aspects of the drugs usable for medical purposes. As heroin, or even cannabis, has an effect on pain reduction there are generalisable action profiles of drugs and their dosages. So when discussing cultural effects of drugs there is a commonly shared profile of experience and cognition gained with the drug that is drug-induced in its mentation. Looking at metaphors used in popular music magazines there is obviously an experience-related body of knowledge among the journalists on using clichés of drug effects (possibly reinforced by their own experiences) to describe the sound design, the musical elements used and the staging of the respective bands and their music. But what is it that Keith Richards described as 'playing his Junkie-Riffs'? What is typical 'Stoner-Music'? Or what is 'the Lyserg-Feeling' in the music of Pink Floyd described by Sheila Whiteley (1997) when analysing the scores of their compositions? Such questions point to a fundamental problem of any culture-based drug research: how should drug effects be inter-subjectively graspable, if not mediated via a shared symbolic frame of reference, that presupposes an internal perspective, an experience on the focused effect discussed? Or as Jimi Hendrix asked with his first record title back in 1967: 'Are You Experienced?'

Shapiro (2003) advocates the thesis that each popular music style in this century was also the expression of a certain lifestyle, to be seen as related to the preferences in drug consumption on the part of the artists and the scene around them who coined this style. From a socio-pharmacological view, the preference of a subculture for a certain drug has always been a kind of fashion to 'turn on', that is to put them into certain physiological conditions in order to experience ordinary and extraordinary events, occurrences and moods more intensively and from a different perspective (Lyttle and Montagne 1992). For example, jazz culture preferred the euphoric plateau of cannabis action, the period of laughter and emotional enjoyment, because it made them 'hot' to play, their auditive impression on music was enhanced and they improvised more expressively (Fachner 2002). Hippy culture seemed to be more interested in the second phase of contemplation and visionary state, as Baudelaire (1994) described the three stages of cannabis intoxication in the middle of the last century. After that, the third phase of vivid hallucinations depends on high doses and a certain set and setting, and is therefore happening between drowsiness, dream states or even sleep. The typical behaviour of the 'stoners' in the second and third stages created the term of 'being stoned', being much too relaxed to move. 'Stoner' cultures, as well as the oriental and Chinese opium smokers, preferred to contemplate recumbently (Jonnes 1999), to be in a perceiving, imagery state, in the state of 'khif' (Gelpke 1982), as referred to in the use of hashish as an intensifier of music perception and production (Fachner 2004a).

Drugs, altered states and music therapy cultures

The use of drugs is predominately reported in the context of addiction. However, there is a culture of using drugs in medical, psychological, traditional and cultural settings, which is not problem-related, and these settings use drugs for certain purposes. For music research and music therapy, these cultures are of interest because they help to understand ways of perceiving and processing music in different states of consciousness.

The connection between music and altered states of consciousness has always been a critical question in terms of public recognition and social perception. Altered state is a term that is, especially in the everyday Anglo-American language, connoted with the state of 'being stoned' or 'being under the influence'. This may irritate those who are not aware of its scientific tradition. The conceptualisation of 'altered states of consciousness' traces back to a long psychiatric and psychotherapeutic discussion that aimed to distinguish (and also to model them for research with psychoactive drugs) states in psychiatric patients, in order to differentiate pathological states in psychosis or other psychopathological processes from healthy altered states that might be used in treatment like music therapy, psychotherapy and also personality development (Aldridge and Fachner 2006).

Early research on music and drugs was published as basic research on music perception, production and therapeutic use (Bonny 1980; Eagle 1972). One research project published in the German area of music therapy by Weber in the 1960s focused on the use of psilocybin, a fungus with psychoactive ingredients (Weber 1974). His work was in the tradition of model psychosis research. The method of a 'model psychosis' was invented to compare psychotic states of hallucination with drug-induced hallucinations and to discuss its noetic and clinical considerations (Gouzoulis-Mayfrank et al. 1998). The aims of this approach are to describe pathological states like the productive states of schizophrenia, which seem to be analogous to some experiences made during psychedelic drug action. In Weber's research, a drug-induced altered music perception should serve as a model of functional regression to earlier levels of cognitive development.

The roots of guided imagery in music go back to the days of LSD (lysergic acid diethylamide) assisted psychotherapy. Helen Bonny conducted the music session in such drug-based psychotherapy research approaches at the Baltimore Hospital, Massachusetts, in the 1960s (Bonny 1980). This research and practice was abandoned when popular culture, and especially the music scene, was seen as using an original pharmaceutical preparation for creative and foremost hedonistic purposes (Fachner 2007). Helen Bonny was urged to use music alone or stop her work. Since she had already discovered that guided imagery in music was as effective as drugs, she continued her music therapy work without those drugs (Bonny 1980).

From the stance of musicology and music therapy, researching emotional aspects of music cognition and performance reveals a growing interest in how music, the brain and consciousness states relate to each other (Levitin 2008), how music is perceived and processed in altered states of consciousness and possible heuristic benefits as a comparison to the so-called 'normal' processes of perception, experience and performance (Blake 2007; Fachner 2006a; Markert 2001; Shapiro 2003; TenBerge 1999). For example, one study measured motor performance and brain activation while playing Erik Satie's *Vexations* for 28 hours. After 15 hours of playing, the pianist reported getting into an altered state. His subjective reports were correlated in brain state changes, as measured with the EEG, and in the music's unstable tempo and loudness, changes were obvious (Kopiez *et al.* 2003). Results showed that executive functions of sensor-motor integration remained stable during trance (Kohlmetz, Kopiez and Altenmüller 2003).

State-dependent recall

Addiction research shows growing interest in how state-dependent recall of music experienced under the influence might serve as cues for drug-related relapses (Esch and Stefano 2004; Forsyth *et al.* 1997; Mays, Clark and Gordon 2008). This is mostly discussed with so-called club drugs like MDMA, ketamine, cannabis, etc. (Becker-Blease 2004; Lofwall, Griffiths and Mintzer 2006; Manning 2007; Moore 2005). Horesh (2006b, 2007b) has gained a lot of data in her work on such processes connected to identity issues and the so-called 'culture of addiction' (White 1996).

As a profession in health care we are dealing more and more with clients exposed to commercialised identity templates offered in the popular music culture. From anthropological research we know that adolescents have to pass through culturally mediated rites of passage (Frith 1998; van Gennep 1986). They have to learn to handle the flowing and changing state of liminality of their being, their senses and their mind, and they have to integrate their first extreme bursts of emotional, sensual and sexual experiences. Some juveniles seek extreme and risky sensations and experiences, in order to expand the role models of their parents and the limitations set by adult society, by checking the boundaries at parties, during binge drinking, heavy drug consumption and other somewhat extreme lifestyle activities preferred to be broadcast and outcast on MTV and other music television channels (Fachner 2004a).

Music therapists like Dijkstra and Hakvoort (2007), Schotsmans (2007) and Punkanen (2006b, 2007) have shown that what is left after such experiences is that music therapy can help restore, find and maintain identities lost in the 'merry-go-round' of ontological uncertainty experienced in post-modern Western societies. Some patients are haunted by traumatic experiences. Some have to be guided through unstable personality states on their biographic journey. But, as time and therapy move on, most addicts learn not to obey the chants of the sirens, as Schotsmans (2007) or Horesh (2006a) allegorise. The sweet call of the sirens was used in old Greek mythology to lure sailors to their death on the rocks through their music and singing.

We also have to be aware that other fields of work like social pedagogics, social therapy, psychotherapy and psychoneuroimmunology apply music and altered states induction procedures to enhance imagery, to support suggestopedia (Lozanov 1978), hypnosis (Meszaros, Szabo and Csako 2002), creative performance (Mellgren 1979), and business success models (Fachner 2006a; Mastnak 1993).

Some people already use music and altered states as a means for personality development, for relaxation, meditation, in the training of mindfulness, in yoga courses, shamanic journeys and in trance experienced at some party nights, and have already developed a certain preference and epistemological stance for the use and action of music and its possible therapeutic benefits (Rill 2006; Rittner 2006; Verres 2007).

Drugs, music and reward

Drugs have different action profiles that may be theoretically categorised according to Julien, Advokat and Comaty (2008) as mainly euphoric, sedative or psychedelic. Euphoric drugs, like cocaine and amphetamines, and sedative drugs, like heroin and tranquilisers, primarily alter the quantity of emotional states. Psychedelic drugs (from the Greek, 'psyche delos' – enhancing consciousness or soul) (e.g. LSD, mescaline, psilocybin) produce qualitative changes in the conceptual-cognitive evaluation of sensory input data. Sedative drugs may help to keep sensory reality in its emotional relation to the perceiving individual at a distance, whereas euphoric drugs eliminate distance almost completely. Psychedelic drugs flood the brain with sensory data and weaken sensory brain functions through contradictory associations of sensory reality (Emrich 1990). A common quality of all psychoactive drugs is that they alter the evaluation of sensory input, its conceptual comparison with known contents and the assessment parameters of (not) relevant information. This happens through drug-specific individual activation and inhibition of the interaction between midbrain, cerebrum and cerebellum. The mesolimbic system of the midbrain that changes the evaluation parameters through emotional colouring of sensory data plays a specific role in this context.

The reward system is receiving more and more attention in science. It has always been in the public interest as it is connected to sensual, emotional and perceptual activity that gives us a 'good' feeling, that changes our mood and focuses our attention on our own body. Eating chocolate or a refreshing drink with some sugar activates the reward system (Small *et al.* 2001). Having sex activates it too and the important cycles of tension and relaxation as Reich has already pointed out (Reich and Wolfe 1945). Climbing a mountain and reaching over the limit of normal capacities mediated via activation of the painkilling opioid system, also known as 'runner's high' (Boecker *et al.* 2008), and even experiencing pain in a religious self-flagellation, makes people strive for situations that are rewarding for them. There are differences in the degree and frequency of striving and fulfilling rewarding bodily activations.

If the frequency of events becomes very high, as observed from lab rats that could not resist receiving the next minutes' electrical activation of their reward centres through a keystroke (Olds and Milner 1954), then the body is in danger even if it is from an overdose of sugar and cacao, three litres of whisky a day or a high dopamine release in getting the next big share from the next complex financial deal.

The global financial crisis that started in 2008 has shown that those who were making big money exhibited the same pattern of loss of control and irresponsibility as addicted drug users. Research has shown that expecting to make monetary profit and being able to possess expensive cultural objects, like expensive sports cars, induces a strong activation in the reward system, namely in the ventral striatum, nucleus accumbens and orbitofrontal cortex (Elliott *et al.* 2003; Erk *et al.* 2002; Knutson *et al.* 2000), areas that influence decision-making processes by valencing expected rewards and their intensity. Some of those crisis-inducing decisions and reward-seeking processes were narrowed to increase profit and to expectations of winning, respect and success in the financial markets, but control over consequences was lost out of sight.

Pleasure and desire

Pleasure, lust and desire are essential evolutionary programmes that guarantee reproduction and satiation and are mediated by the feeling that something good, something that we like, has happened (Esch and Stefano 2004). Pleasure and desire are regulated in different ways. Pleasure is the state in which we feel satiated, happy and well, and is sought. Desire, or lust, is the drive that brings us to this state but has a mechanism of its own.

The dopamine system is active in a tonic and a phasic way. First, the tonic component of dopamine release in the prefrontal cortex of the brain regulates the readiness to react to stimuli. Second, there is an increase in dopamine release (phasic) when meaningful objects are the focus of attention; the more dopamine is released the higher is the personal meaning and valence of the object in focus. All drugs of abuse increase dopamine release and therefore affect these two ways of dopaminergic functioning (Yacubian and Büchel 2009).

Schizophrenic clients were found to display an increased tonic dopamine release. Phasic and tonic dopamine release were decoupled from normal functioning, with the effect that the relevance of stimuli perceived were not differentiated any more or even perceived as meaningful (Abler, Erk and Walter 2005). For a while, scientists were convinced that pleasure was mainly mediated by the dopamine system but then experiments revealed that longing for satisfying experiences, like the taste of chocolate, was still present even when dopamine release was inhibited (Philips 2003). It became obvious that this system was not the only one and that a variety of neurotransmitters and endocrinological communicators were involved (Berridge and Kringelbach 2008). The opioid system, mainly responsible for pain reduction, as well as the endocannabinoid system (Mahler, Smith and Berridge 2007), seem to enhance sensory experience and mediate the feeling of, and therefore endorse the longing for, pleasure (Esch and Stefano 2004).

When it comes to drugs, this separation of pleasure and desire is the most tricky trap for the consumers on their way from drug use to abuse. While the pleasure decreases, or stays the same, with the increased frequency of drug use, the desire for drugs increases correspondingly with the addictive potential of the drug. Addiction research has identified the two 'culprits' for this process of drug sensitisation. While dopamine levels rise after drug ingestion, a protein that serves as a nuclear transcription factor abbreviated as CREB (cAMP [cyclic adenosine monophosphate] response element-binding protein) is released and this leads to a reduced sensitivity of the reward system to the drug. This may sound good so far as it might mean that the sensitivity to the drug is inhibited. But another transcription factor called DeltaFos-B then comes into action and acts like a drug memory concerning the amount of reward the drug has offered (McClung *et al.* 2004). This memory trace increases its somatic impact with the amount of drug use. As the CREB release is terminated straight after drug action, the DeltaFos-B activity, and its according information, stays stable, inducing a memory trace that makes the consumer long for that experience again (Esch and Stefano 2004).

This process of sensitisation also happens with other rewarding pleasure experiences like sex or satiation after food, and is an essential evolutionary process. Behavioural rewards are not mimicking an amount of dopamine, as drugs do it by flooding the nucleus accumbens. Drugs act directly on the neurotransmitter systems of the brain. Therefore, the remaining memory trace is very strong. Opioid and dopamine signal pathways bypass orbitofrontal control functions and the memory traces induced by DeltaFos-B alert the pleasure-seeking system when cues associated with the drug experience are present (Esch and Stefano 2004). If this is a certain music, then desire, then craving and then the long search for satisfaction begins. The same could also be said about playing chess or gardening.

Emotional states, addiction and drug memory

Some people are more vulnerable to drug addiction than others but not all of those who have ever tried drugs become habituated. Yacubian and Büchel (2009) discuss the role of genetically altered dopaminergic tone and neurotransmission that makes people different in their search for or frequency of using certain drugs. Kabbaj *et al.* (2004) discuss the role of neurochemical dysfunctions that might lead 'an individual to seek for a drug of choice to repair that imbalance' (p.112), as it is known from 'hypo-endorphenia' (less endogenous endorphin production) that they may end up in an opiate addiction. Or, it might be a risk-taking and thrill-seeking person or another that uses drugs to cope with environmental stress or has low thresholds to resolve anxiety in social contexts. The idea behind genetic explanation is to seek for the genetic and neural correlates as 'an endophenotype that mediates the likelihood to seek for certain drugs to fulfil this need' (p.112).

Another idea is a self-repair strategy that the brain initiates once it has found the missing substance. It is known that some schizophrenic patients self-medicate with cannabis and a study group showed an imbalance in the brain's endocannabinoid system (Leweke *et al.* 1999). Even when some researchers are convinced that addictive disorders are based on personality traits, as the discussion on premorbidity, genetic disposition (as, for example, revealed with twin studies) or acquired brain disease reflects (Carlezon and Konradi 2004; DuPont 2000; Julien *et al.* 2008; Kabbaj *et al.* 2004; Nestler 2004), the question of, whether we are dealing in treatment with personality states or traits remains an open discussion.

State-dependent perceptual learning processes might resemble those occurring during therapy processes. We can imagine that once a client has experienced, and connected, a primary drug reward with cultural objects and lifestyle in popular culture, the cultural object associated with this lifestyle will be transformed into a secondary reward symbol. Thus, emotional cascades of state-related drug memory will be reactivated when certain cues are heard in the music, or during events in dance, and this may interfere with the aims of therapists. Such problems are not 'in the music', or the substance itself, but connected to the brain reward system, which is linked to perceptual learning and habituation of emotional states like euphoria, flow, joy or pleasantness (Esch and Stefano 2004). Drug-induced positive moods and states of euphoria, listening to preferred music or other pleasing activities like eating, sex or play are mediated through the brain reward system (Julien *et al.* 2008; Small *et al.* 2001).

Patients with a history of drug-induced euphoria may experience a state-dependent recall induced from certain individually perceived cues, which have been experienced together with drugs, as memory traces are stored as conditioned secondary rewards in drug memory (Boening 2001). Research on the state-dependent effects of music on mood and behaviour refers to individual perceptual learning strategies and history under the influence of drug action (Globus *et al.* 1978; Thaut and de l'Etoile 1993). Further research with psychoactive substances and music perception may help to show models of neuro-physiological functions of state-dependent recall and cognition. State-dependent recall of mood and situated cognition is one explanation for the efficiency of music therapy with dementia and Alzheimer's disease patients. Music, and especially songs from adolescence and early adulthood, reactivate memory processes in states no longer accessible by normal daily activities (Aldridge 1994).

However, the connection of joyful experiences intensified by drug action, which produce a strong memory account and craving for such situations, might lead to an addiction. Hereby the addictive potential of different drugs and their specific pharmacokinetic and pharmacodynamic characteristics has to be taken into account. These learning processes have to be focused and transformed in therapy by offering new ways of experiencing.

Music and intense emotions

Intense musical emotions and intoxication appear to have forms of emotional processing in common, at least in regard to reward processing in the limbic system of the brain. Blood and Zatorre's (2001) study demonstrated that highly preferred music that induces chills on the skin of the listener activates the same brain regions as euphoriant drugs like cocaine. Our favourite music interacts directly with structures associated with reward and emotions.

Everybody has a particular musical style or styles that they prefer. Some very special pieces of music may even send shivers down the spine; it is exactly these shivers or chills felt in listening to our favourite music that were used by Blood and Zatorre (2001) to demonstrate that musical information reaches even those brain structures that are involved in conveying emotion. Listening to our favourite melody, we register changes not only in the activity of the autonomic nervous system, heart beat, muscle tension, skin resistance and depth of breathing, but also in the blood flow in brain structures that, according to recent findings, are also involved in processing emotional stimuli. The activation patterns (blood flow) of brain regions (increase: ventral striatum, dorsomedial midbrain, insula, orbitofrontal cortex; decrease: amygdala, left hippocampus, ventromedial prefrontal cortex) show a surprising similarity to activity patterns induced by drugs with a primarily euphoretic effect like cocaine. This similarity suggests that the perception of favourite music interacts directly with structures associated with emotions (Blood and Zatorre 2001).

Reward processes are also physiologically mediated via endogenous neurotransmitters and their corresponding receptor systems, which can be targeted and activated throughout a consumed drug as well. Goldstein (1980) has already shown that the amount of 'chills' can be diminished by administering opioid receptor antagonists such as naloxone to weaken the impact of the emotional experience of music. Opioid receptors with a high density in the brain stem region around the inferior colliculus which 'may mediate attachments we develop to certain beloved sounds' (Panksepp and Bernatzky 2002, p.137) like the voice of the mother, enables us to focus our emotions on certain beloved objects. An intense night in a club under the influence of certain club music and drugs will be remembered and stored as such a beloved sound in the same way and act later as a cue, not for chilling out, but for seeking after those intense events again. Panksepp has described the 'generalised incentive seeking system centred on mesolimbic and mesocortical dopamine circuits' (p.135) that are activated when musical expectancies are coming into play, and is important for the processing of time passages as for rhythmic body movements.

This may help to explain why music has the power to 'intoxicate' individuals who love this particular type of music, and to transport them to an altered state (Fachner 2006a), but when sound processing is stimulated together with mind-altering drugs the above described drug memories seem to be even more potent as they would be with the drug alone.

There is no specific music that has addictive properties but in research on musical emotion it is agreed among cognitive researchers that there is music that represents aspects of basic emotions, like for example sadness, happiness, joy, fear and tenderness (Juslin and Västfjäll 2008; Machleidt, Gutjahr and Mugge 1989). It is also known that some music preferences are distinctively for sad music although it seems like a paradox that sad music can be enjoyable to listen to. What is interesting in terms of chills and their neurochemical basis is the connection to the acoustic properties of the 'separation call' as heard in a high-pitched and sustained crescendo of a singer performing a sad song, such as Meat Loaf's 'For Crying Out Loud, You Know I Love You'. Self-reported chills of participants in this experiment decreased when this particular separation call phrase was notch-filtered about 40 dB at 2, 3 and 4 kHz (Panksepp and Bernatzky 2002). It seems that the experience of being lost and found, to be part of the group's shelter again, is inducing a rush of endorphins when this is expressed acoustically. No wonder that Tsvia Horesh's clients in the therapeutic community were keen to hear this sad Mediterranean music as it was loaded with these separation calls of the singer (Horesh 2006a). The sad music activated the endogenous opioid system and therefore acted as a cue for taking drugs again. Panksepp located this separation-distress circuit experienced in social loss and in certain types of sad music in the 'bed nucleus of the stria terminalis and septal area, the medial diencephalon and the periaqueductal gray matter (PAG)' (Panksepp and Bernatzky 2002, p.144). As separation-distress in birds elevates intracerebral infusions of neuropeptides like oxciticin and prolactin, which subsequently activate the mu-receptor of the opioid family, we may anticipate that music alone, when expressing this separation-distress component of social loss of persons and individually perceived as this expression, may arouse the neuropeptide and opioid system (Panksepp and Bernatzky 2002).

Closing remarks

Drug use is part of Western civilisation, and abuse of drugs, which leads to addiction, affects some people, but not the majority of users. Drugs target and mimic effects of the body's own reward system, binding to appropriate receptors according to their molecular structure and activating dopamine release. This affects the way in which we perceive meaningful content outside and within ourselves. Those who try to break their cycle of distress, enhance creativity, induce altered states of consciousness or target intense hedonistic experiences by using drugs will experience relief and intense emotions for a while, but will risk the likelihood of getting addicted.

Drug use in Western cultures has a long tradition for various purposes, is part of popular culture and a leisure activity. Music is part of the symbolic frame of reference in the rituals of drug use and therefore prone to becoming a cue for addictive behaviour in drug memory. Music appreciation and intense emotions evoked by preferred music activates the reward system and can also induce drug memories of drug use in a music context.

Addiction treatment in music therapy groups can help individuals to experience group cohesion and personal identity without the emotional enhancement of exogenous chemical reward triggering, as the exploitation of endogenous neurochemistry of reward may result in forms of temporary or lasting emotional disorders and brain diseases. Music therapy may help to recalibrate the tonic and phasic dopamine signal-to-noise ratio of emotional intensity differentiation in terms of subjectively meaningful and meaningless information. As enjoying music has to be decoupled from its state-related addiction context, music therapy group processes of music listening and music making, and work on drug memory with songs, can help to relearn the drug-fixation of rewarding emotional experiences. Music therapy can be used as an adjuvant in addiction treatment, showing clients how they can perform in the here and now, helping them feel their bodies in a different way than under the influence of substances, and offering them creative alternatives rather than the rigid strategy of addiction.

CHAPTER 2

Authenticity and Intimacy: The Experience of Group Music Therapy for Substance Dependent Adults Living in a Therapeutic Community

John P. Hedigan

Substance dependence is a widespread phenomenon with damaging consequences that pose significant social problems. The costs are felt by communities around the world, but the most damaging impact of substance dependence is felt by individuals and families. The qualitative research study (Hedigan 2008) described in this chapter used phenomenology to explore the experience of group music therapy for substance dependent adults living in a therapeutic community (Hedigan 2005), with a particular focus on authenticity, relationships and verbal processing of musical experiences. The focus areas stemmed from the researcher's interest in the complex defence mechanisms that substance dependent adults use to avoid intimacy in relationships, and the ways that music can break through these walls which can restrict their capacity for recovery.

Background

Substance dependence

Substance dependence has been described as a chronic, relapsing condition that requires long-term multidisciplinary treatment (Brook 2001; Leshner 1997; Spitz 2001). There are multiple perspectives on addiction pathology including biological, familial, psychodynamic, cognitive-behavioural and societal theories of aetiology (Fals-Stewart, O'Farrel and Birchler 2003; Kooyman 1993; Rotgers 2003). Substance dependence has also been called a 'self-medication' disorder (Kooyman 1993; Murphy and Khantzian 1995) in which addictive behaviours 'compensate for inadequate or overdrawn defences to regulate relationships, sense of self/self-respect, intense emotions, and compulsive/impulsive behaviors' (Ruiz, Strain and Langrod 2007, p.14). Brook (2003) and Flores (2001) have viewed substance abuse as an attachment disorder and Kaufman (1994) has defined the aetiological foundations of substance dependence as including family systems, and childhood and adolescent experiences resulting in affect intolerance. These aetiological complexities require clinicians to approach treatment of substance dependent adults from an eclectic, multi-causal perspective (Vos 1989).

Campling (1999) has described substance dependent adults as having extremely low self-esteem and great difficulty asking for help, as well as being fragile, mistrustful, chaotic and suffering a 'desperate psychic pain' (p.128). Substance dependent adults will often display low self-esteem countered by a grandiose façade, poor understanding and control of emotions, complex defence mechanisms (protective ego systems), and risk-taking behaviours (Brook 2001; De Leon 2000; Kaufman 1994; Kooyman 1993; Treece and Khantzian 1986). Substance dependent adults will often defend themselves by making dishonest statements, by relating from behind a 'mask', or by not engaging in interpersonal relationships openly so as to avoid intimacy where true self-disclosure might occur. The search for interpersonal and intrapersonal authenticity is central to the treatment of substance dependent adults, and to the achievement of positive treatment outcomes.

Authenticity, inauthenticity and the 'false self'

In this study the concept of authenticity refers to an individual's capacity to be genuine and honest with themselves and others. Whitfield (1989) used the term 'true self' to describe who we are 'when we feel most authentic, genuine or spirited' (as cited in Borczon 1997, p.117). Bruscia (1996) states that 'authenticity is being who I am. It is an at-oneness between consciousness, intention, experience and action' (p.105). Laing (1961) gives useful definitions for both authenticity and inauthenticity: 'To be "authentic" is to be true to oneself, to be what one is, to be "genuine". To be "inauthentic" is to not be oneself, to be false to oneself: to not be as one appears to be, to be counterfeit' (p.127).

In his writings about ontological insecurity, Laing (1960) states that in the schizoid individual the self is insecure in its own identity in relation to others, and relates through a 'false self' that attempts to hide this insecurity. Van Deurzen (1998) broadened this view, suggesting that ontological insecurity may be 'essentially there in all of us' (as cited in Cooper 2003, p.104). Winnicott (1965) considered the false self to perform a defensive function that is 'to hide and protect the True Self' (p.142). This idea of a false self refers to the existence of a divide between the inner and outer world, 'the shiny, confident – but false – exterior covering the decidedly less impressive, but real, person within' (Ratey and Johnson 1997, p.160).

Many existentialists have focused on what can be deemed inauthentic rather than what is authentic (Golomb 1995). Heidegger (1962, first published 1926) explained inauthenticity as 'falling into everydayness' or slipping away from our own unique way of being, and into a false way of being in the world that is in accordance with what society expects of us. For Sartre (2003, first published 1943), the importance of authenticity is recognised in its absence. His concept of 'bad faith' described inauthenticity at an intrapsychic level – a lie to oneself. As the 'public self' (the ego) is created, that self is widely exposed to the scrutiny of others. Sartre believed that this process leads us to 'turn to disguises and acts of bad faith' (as cited in Golomb 1995, p.137). Further to this, both Sartre and Heidegger considered 'inauthenticity' and 'bad faith' to be related to the human tendency to attempt to deny and block out of awareness our negative feelings about 'being ourselves', which is a deceptive mode of relating to the self (Cooper 2003).

Substance dependent adults, inauthenticity and avoidance of intimacy

The extent to which substance dependent adults will deny their problems is widely acknowledged in the literature. By means of relating through a false self, substance dependent adults may attempt to avoid and deny the truth about themselves and their problems. Campling (1999) sees that deceit, manipulation and the suppression of information of importance to recovery in the treatment of substance dependent adults require 'urgent attention' (p.136). Wurmser (1985) believes that substance dependent adults use denial to block the perception of painful affects and to deny inner conflicts.

Rotgers, Morgenstern and Walters (2003) have explained this falsity and denial in substance dependent adults as being the reason for addiction treatment being historically confrontational.

The insecurity displayed in relationships by substance dependent adults may be related to avoidance of the intimacy of being 'seen' by others. For Ferrara (1993) intimacy facilitates the 'disclosure and expression of parts of the self that would normally be kept secret for fear of disrupting one's social image' (p.91). In discussing the avoidance of intimacy displayed by substance dependent adults Nathanson (1989) states that 'such a defensive constellation punishes in later life as much as it protects in childhood' (p.51). Being inauthentic makes true intimacy and interpersonal relatedness difficult to achieve. Emotional intimacy is a kind of closeness that must be based on a reciprocal experience of truth, mutuality and understanding. If one behaves inauthentically and is 'loved' for this behaviour, then it is difficult to receive this love in any other way than the false self way it was acquired (Stevens 1971). The intimacy inherent in robust relationships has been described as 'fertile terrain for the development of authenticity' (Ferrara 1993, p.90).

Group psychotherapy and therapeutic community

Group therapy is the most successful and widely used modality in the treatment of substance abuse (Brook 2003; Khantzian, Halliday and McAuliffe 1990; Ruiz *et al.* 2007). Interpersonally oriented group psychotherapy works from the understanding that interpersonal relationships are necessary to 'regulate all aspects of living' (Brook 2003, p.2). When a group is dynamic and functioning well, its productivity is linked to members being authentic with one another (giving and receiving honest feedback), and to a willingness to learn from their interpersonal experiences (Miller 2005; Yalom 1995). Group therapies are useful with substance dependent adults for their dynamic processes that can expose maladaptive interpersonal relating styles (Miller 2005; Yalom 1995). Groups for substance dependent adults can provide opportunities for:

> (a) mutual identification and reduced feelings of isolation and shame;
> (b) peer acceptance, support, and role modelling; (c) therapeutic confrontation and realistic feedback; (d) peer pressure, social support, structure, and accountability for making changes; (e) acquisition of new coping skills; (f) exchange of factual information; and (f) [*sic*] instillation of optimism and hope. (Ruiz *et al.* 2007, p.262)

One of the most intensive forms of group psychotherapy is found within the Therapeutic Community, a model of residential treatment based on a theory of 'community as method' in which all residents are accountable to one another and the values of the facility (De Leon 1997). Therapeutic Communities are drug-free communities in which collective responsibility and 'belonging' are central to treatment success, and residents 'consent to live tighter in an organised and structured setting that facilitates the process of change and the acquisition of a lifestyle free from any form of substance abuse' (Ruiz *et al.* 2007, p.308). Substance dependence is seen as a psychosocial problem that causes disorder of 'the whole person' (De Leon 1997; Lamberti 1999). De Leon (2000) distinguished the Therapeutic Community from other modes of treatment through its 'purposive use of the peer community to facilitate social and psychological change in the individuals' (p.5). The main goal is total abstinence and recovery from substance use, the development of self-awareness and awareness of other, personal growth and the building of positive relationships (De Leon 2000; Kooyman 1993).

Music therapy and treatment of substance dependent adults

Many substance dependent adults are passionate about music, identifying with artists, musical style, and song content. Horesh (2006a) described how her clients feel that music is their 'whole life' and also how many of them 'use' music interchangeably with drugs, to mask or enhance particular feelings and sensations (p.128). Music therapy has been seen as capable of accessing many intrapersonal and interpersonal aspects of the functioning of substance dependent adults (James 1988a; Treder-Wolff 1990b), while also being 'accessible and adaptable for various levels of cognitive, emotional, and physical functioning' (Ghetti 2004, p.89). Music may also be useful to engage treatment-resistant clients by breaking through defences, facilitating communication around common interests, allowing clients to express themselves in new ways, and by increasing self-awareness through facilitating an encounter with the self (Bednarz and Nikkel 1992; Freed 1987; Treder-Wolff 1990a, 1990b; Wheeler 1981).

Music therapy interventions such as songwriting and lyric analysis may be useful for their capacity to share inner or unconscious parts of the client that might otherwise remain hidden (Freed 1987; Gallagher and Steele 2002; Gallant, Holosko and Siegel 1997; Jones 1998; Murphy 1983; Soshensky 2001; Treder-Wolff 1990b). Music may also help substance dependent adults access feelings, an outcome which in turn has been shown to increase self-confidence and self-esteem (Treder-Wolff 1990b; Wheeler

1985). Similarly, song sharing and song discussion may be beneficial for this client population as these interventions may increase awareness of, and the ability to express, feelings (Borczon 1997; Dougherty 1984; Ghetti 2004; James 1988b; Treder-Wolff 1990a).

Stern (2004) considers music therapy to be a psychotherapy that is 'particularly attentive to the "here and now"' (p.142), and goes on to examine the usefulness of such therapies in exposing clinical material that can then be verbalised and explored further. The importance of verbal processing of musical experiences is central to this study. Verbal processing in this context refers to group discussion of an intervention where the therapist elicits immediate reactions from the participants (Bruscia 1987). Nolan (2005) states that this process can allow the dynamics of a group to emerge through discussion of roles played by group members, while also providing 'the opportunity for clients to develop connections between interpersonal events in the music and patterns which occur in their everyday relationships' (p.21). Further to this, Nolan explains that verbal processing of improvisations can facilitate a means by which a client can verbally express previously non-verbal affective states.

Group music therapy has been successfully used in the treatment of substance dependent adults (Dijkstra and Hakvoort 2004; Horesh 2006a; Soshensky 2001). In process-oriented group improvisation:

> The group functions as a laboratory of behaviour and interaction patterns using an affective medium to create a structured environment for practice of feeling expression, socially appropriate behaviour, sensory- and reality-ordered behaviour, and task mastery leading to better self-esteem. (Scovel and Gardstrom 2002, p.186)

While substance dependent adults in residential treatment will normally have extensive experience of different kinds of group processes, music therapy may provide a new and unique way for them to connect and communicate together. Ghetti (2004) describes group music therapy as providing 'a uniquely shared experience that helps overcome the ingrained alienation to which many chronic substance users have become accustomed' (p.89).

Involving substance dependent adults in rhythmic improvisation in groups provides opportunities for communication and interaction with others (Murphy 1983), building group cohesiveness (Gallagher and Steele 2002; James 1988a; Treder-Wolff 1990a), and to counteract isolation and build rapport (Soshensky 2001). Winkelman (2003) found that drumming techniques facilitated pleasurable experiences for substance dependent adults, while also assisting in the reintegration of self and the alleviation of feelings of isolation and alienation by encouraging connectedness. Improvisation may also expose certain dysfunctional behaviours, such as 'not joining in with others, remaining standoffish and doing something on one's own' (Smeijsters 1993, p.228). Group improvisation also allows for exploration and analysis of group dynamics and stimulates the activity of 'group process' (Bednarz and Nikkel 1992; Murphy 1983). Dijkstra and Hakvoort (2004) showed how music can offer opportunities for substance dependent adults to interact in a safe environment, while also providing confronting experiences where they can acutely observe themselves and their issues. Requiring spontaneity, improvisation means participants must 'surrender to a situation that has not been laid down in advance and to find oneself on uncertain ground' (Smeijsters 1993, p.227). This process may challenge the defensiveness of substance dependent adults, an important aspect of many confrontational approaches to treatment of this client group.

Research questions

This study was designed to explore the experience of group music therapy for substance dependent adults living in a therapeutic community. The research questions were devised in line with a phenomenological focus on 'the "how" and "what" of an experience rather than the "why"' (Skewes 2001, p.59). The research questions were divided into two primary questions and three subquestions.

Primary questions

1. What is the experience of group music therapy for substance dependent adults living in a therapeutic community?
2. How does music foster authenticity at an interpersonal level in group music therapy?

Subquestions

1. How do participants describe the interpersonal relationships that are fostered through music?
2. How does music foster authenticity at an intrapersonal level in group music therapy?
3. How does verbal processing assist in deepening interpersonal experiences in group music therapy?

The researcher set out to answer these questions through the experiential descriptions of the participants in the study, with the aim of using the answers to determine the essential features of the experience of music therapy for substance dependent adults.

Method

Phenomenological research

To effectively investigate how substance dependent adults experience group music therapy, as well as their perceptions of how music and dialogue foster authenticity, the method of phenomenology was chosen. Phenomenological research 'directs an intense examination at a phenomenon in an effort to discern the essential aspects of that experience' (Forinash 1993, p.72). Phenomenology finds its modern origins in the work of Edmund Husserl (1859–1938), who developed the paradigm to examine the essence of 'lived experience'. Lived experience refers to the conscious individual experiences humans have in relation to the life events that they experience (Forinash and Grocke 2005). Husserl defined the science of phenomenology as 'the study of the essence of conscious experience' (Smith and Smith 1995, p.9). McKenna (1982, p.178) has explained how Husserl aimed to prove that, through studying perceptual consciousness, researchers can reveal a world of individual experience that can be theoretically understood through scientific inquiry.

Since the 1980s phenomenological research methods have been used effectively in music therapy research. The method lends itself well to studying the subtleties of music therapy, and has the faculty to illuminate complex and mysterious elements of existence (Grocke 1999). Phenomenology was used to explore the experience of a music therapy session during which a patient died (Forinash and Gonzales 1989), and to gather knowledge of patients' experience of music therapy in the terminal stages of illness (Forinash 1990; Hogan 1999). Amir (1990) used phenomenology to explore meaning in improvised songs with a young adult with spinal injuries. More recently phenomenology has been used to explore the experience of listening to music when upset (Racette 2004), and to investigate being effective as a music therapist (Comeau 2004). Phenomenological interviews were used in studies exploring the experience of group music therapy for bereaved adolescents (Skewes 2001), and clients' experience of pivotal moments in the Bonny Method of Guided Imagery and Music (Grocke 1999).

Qualitative interviews

A widely used method for collecting phenomenological data is to conduct qualitative or 'in-depth' interviews to explore an individual's experience of the phenomena in question. Phenomenological interviews are open-ended, give freedom to the interviewer and interviewee, and endeavour to explore and understand the interviewee's experience in depth (Grocke 1999). Kvale (1996) describes a good research interview as proceeding like a normal conversation with a specific purpose and structure, and having a systematic form of open-ended questioning. The interviewer should listen actively to the responses of the interviewee in an effort to sense the possible meanings that are contained within their responses, and should explore these layers of meaning with the subject without the use of leading questions.

The music therapy group

The music therapy group involved eight members of the therapeutic community (the pseudonyms chosen were Brodie, Alice, Phoenix, Irene, Cuba, Anthony, Baggis and Solid) with equal gender representation. Each participant had been in residential treatment for a minimum of five months when they began music therapy, which saw them well-versed in the language of group therapy. Participants took part in ten 90-minute sessions of music therapy (conducted once a week) using the methods of improvisation and song sharing. The music room was well equipped, spacious and provided ample privacy during the music therapy sessions. The music therapy interventions were each followed by extended group dialogue where the participants' thoughts, feelings and relationships were explored. The music therapy group was seen as 'a microcosm of the client's social world where self and interpersonal relationships can be explored and changed' (Bruscia 1987, p.345) and the group's dialogue was both insight- and process-oriented.

IMPROVISATION

The method of improvisation and dialogue can be considered as the Stephens Model of Adult Improvisation. This model features the integration of musical and verbal techniques, and improvisation is seen as capable of 'revealing both symbolic and actual aspects of interaction' (Bruscia 1987, p.335). The instruments available included tuned percussion (alto metallophone, bass xylophone), a selection of untuned percussion (djembes, bongos, conga, log-drum, dun-dun, guiro, shakers, tambourines, bells, repeniqué, maracas, agogo, wood blocks, castanets, finger cymbals) and a large bass drum (a Brazilian surdo). The group's improvisations were non-referential, and remained entirely spontaneous and undirected. Musically they could be described as being tribal sounding at times, dynamically varied, and featuring many layers of rhythm and melody. Over the duration of the ten sessions the participants experimented with different instruments and ways of communicating musically, and through this experimentation they broadened their palette of sound considerably. The improvisations normally lasted between 8 and 12 minutes.

SONG SHARING

Group improvisation was followed by a song sharing intervention where in each session a single song was shared by one member of the group. Song sharing has also been called song analysis, compact disc sharing, song lyric discussion, and song-based discussion (Grocke and Wigram 2007). Group members had a number of weeks to choose a song that had meaning for them, and that would potentially share something significant with their peers. The songs shared included songs by Australian artists Missy Higgins and Pete Murray, as well as songs by John Lennon, Moby, Staind, Soundgarden and Evanescence. Themes explored through these songs included death, emptiness, isolation, depression, resentment, disguises, desperation and hope. The group listened to each song together while viewing the lyrics to absorb as many aspects of the songs as possible. Forty-five minutes was allocated for each session's song during which the group member had the opportunity to share why they chose the song, and the group could respond with their own thoughts, questions and insights.

Data collection

The raw data in this study comprised individual in-depth interviews conducted with the purpose of exploring each participant's experience of group music therapy. The interviews were based on a pre-planned set of questions designed to assist the interviewee in the pursuit of a detailed description of their experience. Most importantly the researcher avoided leading questions and made use of broad and open-ended questions (e.g. 'What was it like for you to be a part of the music therapy group?') where participants were given the freedom to let their responses sprawl in a variety of directions that were important to them. The interviews (recorded on an iRiver MP3 player) were conducted in the two weeks following the final session and took place in the music room.

Data analysis

This study aimed to find the essence of how the participants experienced group music therapy, and to explore their perceptions of the effect of musical experiences and group dialogue on authenticity and relationships. The 'protocols' (complete transcribed interviews) are the starting point for phenomenological analysis. Phenomenological data analysis aims 'to derive from the collection of protocols…a description of the essential features of that experience' (Polkinghorne 1989, p.50). Phenomenological reduction, also called distillation, sees data broken down into manageable units of meaning that assist in finding the essence of an individual's experience (the individual essence).

The procedure of analysis and reduction used in this study, based on Grocke's (1999) method, was undertaken one protocol at a time and is outlined in eight steps, broken into two stages. The first stage is shown in the following six steps:

1. Multiple readings of the protocol.
2. Identification of key statements related to the experience of the group.
3. Extraction of key statements.
4. Key statements grouped into meaning units with category headings.
5. Meaning units inform the writing of a distilled essence of the participant's experience of group music therapy.
6. Participant reads their protocol, meaning units and individual essence and verifies whether they think it is an accurate description of their experience of music therapy. Changes are made if requested.

MEANING UNITS (EXAMPLE)

For clarity, an example is included of what a meaning unit looks like when extracted from a protocol. The heading indicates the unit's category heading, and grouped with it are the statements that make up the meaning unit:

Improvisation gave Irene opportunities to feel connections with others

- 'There's moments when you're in an improvisation where you can just feel the connection that's happening…I felt completely connected. They're really significant moments for me.'
- 'As in any group when you're that intimate with each other you do have a connection from it.'

- 'The feel I have from the improvisations is they always meshed somewhere…for me I found that connection.'
- 'The group taught me a lot about this medium of connecting with people.'

This is simply an example of one stage of phenomenological reduction as undertaken in this study. There were often many more meaning units under each category heading derived from a protocol, and each had many category headings. Once all the meaning units were completed, they were used to create the individual essence of the participants' experience by 'tying them together' into a logical and clear flow (Polkinghorne 1989, p.55).

Global analysis and identification of global themes

The last stages of analysis and reduction drew upon parts of the results generated by the process of distillation of the individual essences. This is shown in the final two steps:

7. Global analysis where the meaning units are examined for common themes (i.e. themes that are repeated across the eight protocols).
8. Global themes inform the writing of the final global essence of how the eight participants experienced group music therapy.

Global analysis was achieved through finding the meaning units that were common across the experience for the participant's, and grouping these together as global themes. The process involved identifying a meaning unit in one protocol that was key to the experience of that individual and then looking across all the other participants' meaning units to see if they had made related statements. The global themes were developed to find a view of the data that illustrated the meaning units that were discussed by all eight participants in the study, then meaning units for seven, and then six, and so forth, down to those that were unique to the experience of an individual participant. Once the researcher had examined all related statements under a particular category, the most appropriate synthesis of these statements was used to create the wording of the global theme (often taken from the clearest description of one of the participants). Once the global themes had been identified and organised into a manageable format, these units were divided into major, frequent and minor categories:

1. **Major themes**: These were units of meaning discussed by six, seven or all eight participants. The study found 17 major themes.

2. **Frequent themes**: These were units of meaning that were discussed by three, four or five of the participants. The study found 35 frequent themes.

3. **Minor themes**: These were units of meaning that were discussed by two participants, or units of meaning that were unique to the experience of an individual participant. The study found 27 minor themes.

Results of the study

Major themes

The major themes were drawn from the meaning units discussed by six, seven or all eight participants in the study. Listed below are the six global themes which were common to all eight protocols.

- Participants made connections with each other through their weekly improvised music.
- Improvisation was an exposing experience that brought down defences and revealed the participants to one another.
- The music therapy group was experienced as challenging, uncomfortable, awkward and confronting.
- The music therapy group was intimate and developed closeness in the relationships between the participants.
- The music therapy group brought out honesty, genuineness and the 'real' sides of people.
- The experience of the group deepened participants' understanding of themselves and their relationships.

Global essence

The 17 major themes were used to create the global essence of the experience of substance dependent adults in a music therapy group. This process was achieved by placing these themes together and writing them in prose. The global essence sees over 40,000 words of protocols reduced to a 230-word global essence of the experience of the group, and represents the essential results of the study:

The music therapy group was an intimate experience that developed closeness with others. It brought out honesty, genuineness and the 'real' sides of people. The experience deepened self-understanding and the understanding of relationships with others. The group provoked feelings of discomfort, with some aspects described as challenging, uncomfortable, awkward and confronting. Seeing and hearing that others in the group shared the same discomfort made it easier to be honest about personal discomfort.

Improvisation and song sharing generated challenging feedback that was considered therapeutically productive. These activities, in conjunction with the group's dialogue, helped the group members to be open with each other, enabling them to speak their thoughts and feelings with confidence and clarity. Improvising music together promoted self-consciousness and there was a risk of feeling embarrassed or looking silly. This was an exposing experience that brought down defences and revealed the group members to one another, while also helping them to connect. Eye contact made while improvising was described as intimate, confronting and challenging. Song sharing deepened the knowledge of others.

In contrast to its challenging and confronting qualities, the music therapy experience was also enjoyable and fun. There was a gradual evolution to the group and the experience became increasingly comfortable with time. Seeing others taking risks and actively struggling with therapeutic issues was inspirational. The personal gains made in music therapy had a lasting effect beyond the group's duration.

The findings of this study are in the rich statements made by the participants about their experience of the music group, most particularly those that relate to the research questions. These are answered here, using the descriptions gathered in the interviews.

Discussion

Authenticity and intimacy

All participants felt the music therapy group was an intimate experience that developed closeness with others. A number of factors can be seen as having influenced this experience of intimacy, including the use of music, and the confronting and revealing qualities of the music interventions. For Cuba, the musical connections brought the participants together. He said that the 'most amazing part of it [the group experience] was to feel connected and intimate in that space...maybe that was as well through the connections through the music'. Irene felt that the improvisation and dialogue was 'confronting' and for her 'when something's confronting you can't hide any more...and that's where I think the intimacy comes from'.

All of the participants made statements indicating their experience of honesty, genuineness and the 'real' sides of people in the music therapy group. Cuba described the group as 'very honest', and how 'hearing people's honesty and feedback just brought me into that world of being connected in a relationship and everything that brings'. Solid said he 'could see people were more genuine in the moment' in the group. Alice felt that closeness in relationships was generated by 'honesty in the group'. Four participants described how the group's improvising brought out 'the real side' of other participants. Solid said he 'could see people were more genuine in the moment' in the group. Alice felt that closeness in relationships was generated by 'honesty in the group'.

Challenging, uncomfortable, awkward and confronting

Many aspects of the participants' experience of music therapy were difficult for them. Each felt the group provoked feelings of discomfort, with some aspects described as challenging, uncomfortable, awkward and confronting. Phoenix explained how 'at the beginning I really didn't enjoy [it] at all. I just felt so self-conscious. I found it really difficult to just let myself go.' Brodie said that 'in the first week I couldn't look at anyone. I was really uncomfortable.' Cuba pointed out that in the early sessions 'everyone felt really uncomfortable with the music making' and connecting with others was 'almost painful, it was that uncomfortable'.

Enjoyable, fun and safe

In contrast to its challenging and confronting qualities, the group was also described by six participants as enjoyable and fun. Irene said she 'really enjoyed the musical aspect' of the group and that once she got over her initial resistance 'it just felt so good'. Baggis felt the achievement of finding comfort in the group was important because 'it turned out to be fun'. Five participants described feeling safe in music therapy. Anthony felt that 'once everyone realised it was a safe environment...everyone realised what the benefit was of letting those actual walls down'. Cuba explained music's role in creating this feeling of safety, saying, 'It's music and it's safe and you don't have to sort of go in there thinking, "I've got to watch out that this behaviour doesn't come out."' When Irene shared her song, which carried memories about the suicide of a friend, she explained that she felt both vulnerable and safe. 'Even though that was the most vulnerable I was in the group, I actually felt safe in doing that. I didn't feel the need to shut down and hold it in.'

Freedom

Five participants described improvisation as giving them the opportunity to let go and express themselves freely in the music. Irene explained that she 'found a lot of spontaneity in it to be creative in a free way'. Phoenix felt a sense of freedom in the improvisations that was 'like flying. It was just that sense of freeness. Free from myself. Free from my worries, my thoughts [and] expectations.' Phoenix added, 'What I remember most is that, probably the last couple of sessions, when I just really enjoyed myself and I felt really free playing the instruments.' Brodie described a similar feeling, that improvisation gave her the chance to feel free from her need for control, 'to just be' and be 'able to let go'. After struggling at first, Solid explained that he eventually felt a 'real sense of freedom and liberation' to express himself musically and verbally in the group's dialogue.

How music fosters interpersonal authenticity

Improvisation brought down defences

All of the participants described improvisation as an exposing experience that brought down defences and revealed the participants to one another. Brodie described improvisation as like 'being stripped bare' and 'baring your soul'. While discussing improvisation Irene explained that:

> Because it's a foreign way of communicating, a lot of what happens happens without you consciously realising that you still are communicating and you still are experiencing and expressing the emotions that you would if you were actually speaking it.

Here Irene indicates her perception that music provides a way of revealing the participants to one another in fashion that is out of their control. Alice supported this view, describing her sense that she saw the real side of Phoenix because Phoenix 'had no control over the music'. Alice explained that improvisation exposed the participant's interpersonal traits because while playing 'they're unconscious of them. You're diverted from what you're trying to control in yourself by the music. You're not on guard. Your guard's let down at various moments and that's why things come out.' Alice further explained that while improvising 'you give more of yourself because you don't have time to manufacture something else', suggesting that the spontaneity of improvisation makes it difficult to remain defended.

Participants experienced honesty, genuineness and the 'real' sides of people

Each participant felt that the group brought out honesty, genuineness and the 'real' sides of people. These qualities are considered to be within the study's definition of authenticity. Cuba felt the group gradually became 'more and more honest'. For Solid, 'As time went by we all kind of got better at it. I could see that people were more genuine in the moment.' Brodie described 'feeling a lot more real' in the group. Closely related to this 'realness' that music may have fostered in the participants is the possibility that authentic self-disclosure may make it easier for others to relate authentically. Three participants found it easier to connect when others had their guard down and were being real. Baggis felt that 'it does help me [connect] 'cause it makes things real, if I can see a realness to it'. Brodie described a moment where Alice shared herself emotionally with the group as 'beautiful, just watching her do that, seeing the façade slip away'.

Five participants felt that the dialogue generated by improvisation was something that challenged their guardedness in the group. During the group's dialogue around improvisation, Irene felt 'emotionally naked just sitting there'. Irene further explained how group feedback often meant she could not be 'as guarded as I like to be', indicating that improvisation and dialogue challenged her to be authentic with others by getting beyond her guardedness. This may be because participants feel so exposed by the process of improvising that they feel it would be difficult to deny what they think their peers have already 'seen' in them.

How relationships are fostered through music

All of the participants described the music therapy group as intimate, and felt that the experience developed closeness in their relationships. Baggis indicated that the group's music 'brought everyone closer'. Alice said, 'I'm a lot closer to the people that are in music therapy than I am to other people in my peer group. So that has to be a reflection on the music.' Cuba felt the group 'was definitely intimate. I definitely found intimacy.' Brodie said, 'We were certainly getting to know each other. It's had a completely positive effect [on my relationships].' All eight participants said that they made connections with others in the weekly improvisations. These connections made while improvising appear to have had an impact on the participants' relationships. Referring to these, Irene said, 'There's moments when you're in an improvisation where you can just feel the connection that's happening…I felt just completely connected.' All the participants also felt that the group deepened their understanding of their relationships. Irene said, 'Those relationships in here have come a long way since I've started music therapy.' Anthony said, 'I can see even the difference in them [my relationships]. With a lot of people in that group I certainly feel closer to and more connected with.' Cuba commented that 'the most amazing part [of the group] was to feel connected and intimate'.

How music fosters intrapersonal authenticity

Seven participants made statements related to feeling self-conscious while improvising and also felt there was a risk of feeling embarrassed or looking silly. Brodie said, 'I was too concerned with what I was playing, that it wasn't going to sound OK, there's embarrassment there. [I was] doubting myself.' Phoenix said, 'Playing the instruments helped me to be able to look at my own thought processes.' When talking about the exposing nature of improvisation, Solid described feeling 'agonisingly awkward'. Cuba indicated that he could not avoid the realities that improvisation presented to him about his discomfort with connection and intimacy, saying he 'found you just couldn't hide. You couldn't hide things from yourself.'

It has been previously described how the participants felt that improvisation was an exposing experience. It is possible that the intimacy of the group and its confronting nature had the effect of enhancing the impact of intrapersonal realisations, because they occurred within an exposing and open group forum. This type of self-consciousness may indicate that group music therapy provokes an awareness of oneself. Four participants felt the experience of the group deepened their understanding of themselves while three felt that improvisation made them look at their own thought processes. Phoenix provides an explanation of this process, saying that:

> Playing the instruments helped me to be able to look at my own thought processes and sometimes I don't really understand why I'm feeling a certain way…or what the feelings are, but through music I was able to discover what it is and able to articulate it.

Here Phoenix demonstrates how improvisation provoked feelings and insights that were intrapersonally authentic for her, after which she had the opportunity to discuss these in a group setting.

How verbal processing deepens interpersonal experiences

Six participants felt that the group's musical activities generated challenging feedback that was therapeutically productive, something that challenged their guardedness in the group. Brodie felt that the processes revealed in the group's dialogue 'put our relationships to the test, to see how far we were willing to go, and willing to trust each other'. To be able to talk about her own thoughts and processes, Brodie had to 'put down all my defences' and hearing feedback was

> confronting definitely, but it was also good to hear people actually tell me [about their experience of me]…When it comes to anything confronting a lot of people shy off from it, so that was really good 'cause it's something I really need.

Here Brodie indicates the importance of verbal processing of her own experiences in music therapy. It is possible that, without the process of dialogue after music, Brodie may have learned little about how others experienced her. Cuba explained that verbal processing allowed the participants to challenge each other around what improvisation revealed, saying that 'people would get feedback…and be sort of challenged to maybe step out of that role'. For Baggis, improvisation was a way of 'opening yourself up to scrutiny' by the other members of the group. Irene stated, 'You'd express something in the music and you'd get the feedback about it and more often than not it would be like really relevant to something that was going on.'

Six participants said that hearing others verbally reveal the discomfort they experienced in response to the music therapy interventions was something that made it easier to be honest in the group. For Baggis there was 'a shared uncomfortability that we all sort of had'. He felt glad to 'hear other people are going through the same thing and knowing that I wasn't the only one that felt as uncomfortable'. Brodie said:

> I can see other people doing it and I think 'well maybe it is OK to be that open and honest'…Seeing them not rejected or not feeling hurt, and seeing the courage that people show, helps and enables me to do the same thing.

Phoenix said:

> I guess one thing I've learnt is we all sort of have the same anxieties and worries and things like that even though I don't think we talk about it much…but we were able to in music therapy. We pretty much all had the same insecurities.

This reciprocity of interpersonal sharing is considered a robust answer to the question of how verbal processing assists in deepening interpersonal experiences in group music therapy. Without verbal processing of the experiences in improvisation, participants may have been left thinking that they alone had felt discomfort. Through verbal processing of the experience it was revealed that this feeling was common in the early stages of the group.

Emergent themes

Safety and confrontation

There is great importance in the fact that music therapy was experienced with these sharply contrasting feelings. This dichotomy provides balance to the experience for the participants, keeping the group therapeutically challenging but also making it, to some extent, user-friendly. If the group was not fun, it may have been so confrontational that the participants' capacity to be authentic was disabled. If the group was experienced as only fun and non-confrontational then the participants may have not learned as much as they did about the nature of self and other. Because improvisation was experienced as confronting and exposing, the participants each had the valuable experience of working through their difficulty to the point where the experience was not only tolerable, but enjoyable.

Eye contact

The experience of eye contact during improvisation as being confronting was a major global theme in this study, though its discussion requires some interpretation because of its intersubjective nature. Seven participants described eye contact made while improvising as being intimate, confronting and challenging. Making eye contact during improvisation may be linked to authenticity because of the deeply intimate contact that it creates. Cuba described his difficulty with eye contact, saying, 'At the start it was just about realising how uncomfortable I was with connecting with people and that would just be through eye contact.' Baggis felt it was 'confronting to look someone in the eye when you're playing something you're not really comfortable playing…You don't even have to say anything and it's more uncomfortable than speaking to someone.' Irene explained that eye contact is important 'because you're doing it together then. It completes the connection. You might be playing together but when you have that eye contact it becomes the two of you. And the intimacy of course.' Irene may be suggesting that eye contact 'completes a connection' through creating a deeper intersubjective knowing between participants.

Improvisation reflects personalities, moods and relationships

Five participants made statements related to their sense that their improvised music helped them to communicate with each other about their relationships through the fact that the music itself was reflective of those relationships. Because the improvisation was used in conjunction with group dialogue about the experience, this meant that the participants had the chance to speak about their sense of each other gained through the music making. In each session, this generated valuable feedback that was grounded in the 'here and now'. Cuba felt that while improvising 'you're not protecting yourself…you're just open, you're just doing what you normally do, you just interact how you normally interact'. Baggis said:

> You could look at someone playing and either see them smiling or not even looking at anyone and determine just from that that they're in this kind of mood and that gets me thinking 'alright they were like this earlier today and they're a bit like this' and all you need to do is question someone vaguely on it and a lot more comes out.

Solid said:

> Heaps of what we were doing could be applied to our relationships and how we are relating to each other… It's an in-your-face demonstration of…something you're doing in a relationship. Like an abstract way of representing other things that you're doing.

Conclusions

This study explored the experience of group music therapy for substance dependent adults living in a therapeutic community, with a particular focus on authenticity, relationships and verbal processing of musical experiences. It was found that music therapy is experienced as an exposing treatment modality that can potentially break down the defences of substance dependent adults, while also stimulating productive, relationship-based dialogue which provides an opportunity for authentic interpersonal relating. In the light of the fact that treatment of substance dependent adults is historically confrontational, music therapy may be a well-indicated treatment for this client group. Given this study's phenomenological method, and its focus on presenting the authentic voice of each participant's experience, it seems appropriate to finish with the words of a participant. Here, Irene describes the way that music therapy can break through the defences of substance dependent adults, and bring them into an intimate interpersonal field where true authentic relating can assist in their recovery from substance dependence.

> For me when something's confronting you can't hide any more. And in not being able to hide people are seeing the truth. When improvising you're not able to use the façade or use your words to hide behind, or to manipulate or trick. I think when people get such a genuine sense of you that's really confronting. I think that's where the intimacy comes from.

CHAPTER 3

Drug Addicts and Their Music: A Story of a Complex Relationship

Tsvia Horesh

Introduction

Working as a music therapist in drug addiction rehabilitation centers in Israel, I have come across many clients who have spoken about the music in their lives. Their music holds many important emotional and social functions for them. It is intertwined, directly or indirectly, with issues they must deal with in therapy.

In many rehabilitation centers, I have found a limited awareness of the need to work with addicts on their relationship with their music. There does seem to be an awareness of the negative effects some genres of music have on recovering addicts, to the point where these genres are forbidden to be listened to during treatment. The choice of genres censored is culturally dependent and will be different depending on the cultural and ethnic origins of the clients.

This censorship possibly passes a non-explicit message to the clients that this music is dangerous for them and they must relinquish it in order to recover from their addiction. However, many addicts see their music as an integral and important part of their lives, and will not give it up easily. Upon finishing their treatment, after months of being separated from their music, many of them will be drawn, with great yearning, back to their drug abuse-related music. They will have little or no awareness of the complex meanings this music has for them, apart from the fact that it is "bad" for them.

Many of my clients, speaking about their music, say that "music is my life"; but the music in their lives does not always reflect positive aspects. The music in their lives has played, for some of them, a significant part in their self-destructive, obsessive behavior. Their lives—and the music in their lives—are not harmonious. Many claim to have lost control over their emotions and behavior after listening to music.

My incentive to research this issue was to uncover and understand the many faceted meanings that music has in drug addicts' lives. I was driven to understand the different forces I felt were lurking behind this phenomenon. My qualitative research project was conducted as a master of arts research student at the Hebrew University in Jerusalem, Israel, and was based upon the analysis of eight narrative interviews with drug addicts who had participated in my music therapy groups.

All the informants mentioned in this chapter agreed to be portrayed in this research. All were given pseudonyms. They are all graduates of therapeutic communities and at the time of the interview abstained from drug and alcohol abuse. Of the eight people interviewed for my thesis, I have chosen to bring here the voices of six of them.

The research was conducted in the qualitative–narrative method. The narrative method strives to understand the world of human experience from the viewpoint of the people living their experience and telling about it. The recorded and transcribed interviews were treated as original texts and were analyzed according to a hermeneutic train of thought. In the spirit of the narrative method, the words of the informants (translated from Hebrew) are brought to illustrate the different subjects dealt with in this chapter.

This chapter summarizes selected findings from my research, and includes insights from my clinical experience. Other and related findings of this research have been published elsewhere (Horesh 2006a, 2006b, 2006c, 2007a, 2007b).

The therapeutic community and its clients

The basic ideology of the therapeutic community is one of inclusive, drug-free, therapeutic care for the addict as an individual and as a member of society. This ideology is based on the assumption that drug dependency is a mix of educational, psychosocial, medical, emotional, spiritual, and psychological factors, all of which must be addressed by treatment. It incorporates both psychodynamic and behavior-modification methods in an effort to relate to the complexity of the issues of addiction.

My clients are addicted to drugs and/or alcohol, undergoing an inpatient treatment program in the Ramot–Yehuda–Zoharim therapeutic community, in Israel. The men and women in this therapeutic community are aged between 19 and 55 years, with a history of drug abuse lasting between 2 and 40 years. The majority have lived a life of crime and may have spent time in prison. Many come from multi-problem families, with a history of various addictions and life in crime-ridden neighborhoods. About half of our clients are Jewish, Israeli born, second or third generation descendants of immigrants from Arab countries. Forty percent of our clients are immigrants from the former Soviet Union and have been living in Israel for 20 years or less. Ten percent are Palestinians holding Israeli citizenship.

The work with clients and their experiences

In our music therapy groups we listen together to music from the clients' childhood, adolescence, and drug-abusing years. We validate and contain the emotions, memories, and life stories the music evokes. We discuss, negotiate, and re-evaluate their relationship with the music. For many of the people these sessions enable them, for the first time, to examine their relationship with their music—the "soundtrack of their lives"—in the secure and containing environment of the group. This is a chance to observe how the music defines their personal, social, and ethnic identity; how they use music in their daily lives; how their music relates to their drug abuse; and what dangers or risks it holds for them. The final stage is to discover how music can function as an integral part of their recovery, and as a source of relaxation, joy, and well-being.

In one session a Russian-born client brought a ballad by Anathema, a heavy metal group, with a text about loneliness and depression. Another client, of North African descent, brought his Middle Eastern style music, a song with lyrics depicting similar emotions. Needless to say, each of the clients did not enjoy listening to the other's music, and my request to "suffer through" the songs politely made for some tension in the group. But in the ensuing discussion, each client was able to connect to the other's depressive position, as depicted in each song, although in very different musical and cultural ways. They both found their searches for validation of their depression in their respective song's lyrics to be similar. They also realized that the effect the music had on their emotional state—each client relating to his specific genre—was similar.

Psychodynamic aspects of music listening

Music listening as a transitional phenomenon

The abuse of drugs, at the beginning stages, is often motivated by the need to reduce anxiety, the drugs serving as a container, processor, and filter. But, instead of becoming a transitional object, the substance becomes the object itself—and dependency is formed. There is no room for individuation and separation from the drug, no ability to discern the boundaries between 'me' and "not me". The dependency becomes addiction, which leads the addict into a regressive state.

Nahum relates how he used music, during his drug-abusing years, as a source of containment, consolation, comfort—and refuge:

> I had to escape, I couldn't stay in my…not so good reality. So you listen to music, as a sort of place to hide in, where you can go to this wonderful, make-believe world…You're asking how music and drugs are connected? Why you need the music? So as not to be alone… my soul is crying out, I can't understand what's going on with me, I don't want to be like this. At first the drugs were for fun, but then they became a need, a very very deep physical and spiritual need. An almost total lack of ability to function in all parts of my life…but I didn't want to see it. I didn't want all this quiet around me, it reminded me how lonely I was, how I was ruining my life. So…the music comes, doesn't matter what you listen to…it was a very strong dependence.

Lehtonen (2002) suggests that music seems to create a symbolic distance between the individual and their traumatic experiences, probably because of music's ability to act as a transitional phenomenon, whereby listening to music one can safely and without anguish work through one's feelings. He quotes Racker (1951) who described the qualities of music as a transitional phenomenon. Music can protect an individual against unpleasant feelings and yet, at the same time, give psychic strength to face and overcome them. Music can also be used in frightening and unpleasant situations, for instance against silence representing loneliness. Music can function as a "mirror" where the listener sees themselves and their inner, incoherent feelings and experiences—in an integrated state.

Nahum added: "I would sit and really listen to the music; when I felt down I listened to sad, dark music... I tried to see where I was and what I was doing with my life."

Nahum described a two-way process. On one hand, he wanted to escape the feelings of loneliness and failure, and so listened to music. On the other hand, he wanted to reflect his depression and so—listened to sad music. Nahum's experience is validated by Frith (1987), who writes that music can enable the enjoyment of emotion—even if that emotion is anger or sadness. Music allows one to be immersed in the emotion, while at the same time keeping a safe distance from it. The music, as a transitional phenomenon, enables one to connect and to distance simultaneously. It dwells in the intermediate space that is inhabited by images, from the outer, as well as from the inner, reality.

Regressive transitional phenomena

Dima and Yelena spoke about their own dependence on music:

> Dima: "I can't imagine myself without music...there's no way I'll give it up."

> Yelena: "Music was with me 25 hours a day, I couldn't stand being without music."

It seems that here we are looking at a phenomenon based in the very early stages of attachment. The music has the properties of a primary object and losing touch with that object causes anxiety (Winnicott 1984). The relationship with music, as described by Dima and Yelena, is one of dependency, and possibly similar to their relationship with their drugs. They will both go to great lengths so as not to be without music. Music listening as an intensive pastime—to the degree that it could be seen as a transitional phenomenon—is characteristic of adolescence (Lull 1987; Sugarman and Jaffe 1987). The relationships described by most of the informants (aged 20–40) with their music are similar in their intensity and significance to those of adolescents.

We can, therefore, speculate that some of the informants' listening habits function as arrested, non-flexible, non-chronological transitional phenomena, a relic from their adolescent years, usually the period of initial drug abuse. My clinical observations have shown that, in addition to music-listening behavior, some other social behavior portrayed by my clients are reminiscent of adolescence. It seems that extensive drug abuse, beginning in adolescence, may prevent normal maturation into early adulthood. We can conclude that the relationships the informants formed with their music feed from the same deprivations, needs, and impulses that are at the core of their relationships with their drugs. These unique attachments with music have addictive characteristics.

Regression and symbolic distance

Some of the informants spoke about the actual damage they felt that their music caused them, during difficult periods of their lives.

Zohar said: "When my [drug] using was really bad, I would listen to these sad songs, this guy singing about how he's all alone…I mean, you can go crazy…it's like I enjoyed suffering, it was like masochistic. I don't know what to call it—it was like hurting myself on purpose, hitting myself when I felt bad." He continued: "I had to release what I felt so I listened to all those songs that told about guys like me, where he really sings about what he feels…"

Yelena spoke about what she called "her dangerous music". She saw a clear connection between the music she listened to during her drug and alcohol abusing years, and the self-abuse she inflicted upon herself:

> There were situations where some of the music I listened to seemed to attack me…all the harm I did to myself—was with the music. It was during drugs, and depression and alcohol… I listened to that music and it was as if somebody was sitting and talking to me…and saying that everything is wrong and bad and there's no point in living… There are lots of songs like that… I don't think that I would have had the guts to hurt myself the way I did, without that music… I would listen to the music, get even more depressed, and cry, and walk around feeling bad all day.

Both Zohar and Yelena spoke about a regressive experience while listening to their music: the almost total absence of boundaries between themselves and the music, a complete identification with the songs' textual and musical messages.

How can we comprehend such a high sensitivity to music? What compels these drug addicts to choose to listen to music that they know will cause them suffering? What need does this form of self-abuse fill?

Let us step back a moment and see how Aaron Copland describes music's unique properties, actually relating transitional phenomena attributes:

> There is something in music that keeps it as if at a distance even at the moment when taking us into its embrace. It is simultaneously absent

outside us and yet it is an inner part of ourselves. Even though it shakes us profoundly it is all the time under our control. It leads us forward but for some reason we never lose control. (Copland 1952 in Lehtonen 2002, p.78).

Kohut and Levarie, in their psychoanalytical discourses on music listening, described the

oceanic feeling one may achieve by listening to music. The listener and the music become "one" emotionally. The ecstatic listener does not clearly differentiate between himself and the outside world—he experiences the sounds as being produced by himself...emotionally they are what he feels...the ability to regress to this early ego state, while at the same time preserving the complicated ego functions required to recognize and master the influx of organized sound, is the prerequisite for the enjoyment of music. (Kohut and Levarie 1990, p.19)

These perspectives on music listening may partially explain Zohar's and Yelena's experiences described above. Indeed, there is no true enjoyment of the music, but there is clearly a regression to a state of lack of distinction and absence of boundaries between one's self and the music. Over-identification with the music can bring one to a situation of engulfment or, figuratively, of "drowning" in the ocean of emotional regression.

But both quotes speak about organizing and containing factors, that should keep the listener, so to speak, "above water": Copland stresses controlling abilities activated by the music, and a symbolic distance activated by the listener, and Kohut and Levarie mention complicated ego functions which master the influx of sound, while enabling the regression to early states. It seems that these factors are not accessible to my informants, who describe disturbing and frightening experiences brought upon by listening to music, under certain circumstances.

The music does not always function as a transitional phenomenon, aimed at keeping the traumatic memories and associations, aroused by the music, at a safe distance. It seems that, sometimes, the music is the raw emotion itself—and not a symbol of the emotion. The music *is* the trauma, the original pain, the abyss, the anger—and the only reality one can perceive.

It is possible that the actual effects of the different drugs on cognitive, emotional, and physiological functions may play a part in this over-sensitivity to music. All psychoactive drugs alter the evaluation of sensory input, its comparison with known contents, and the assessment parameters of non-relevant information. The biochemical and neurological effects of certain drugs, mainly hallucinogenics and cannabis, include the deletion of the natural perception barriers of the brain and can bring about sensory overload (Fachner 2006b). It may be possible that these effects can bring about deterioration of the symbolic distance, and of the high ego functioning, mentioned above.

In addition, we may look for explanations in the emotional and personality characteristics of the informants, and the psychological dysfunction displayed by many addicts. This dysfunction is partly the result of the drug abuse. It seems that some aspects of personality disorders apparent in addicts' behavior have developed secondarily as a consequence of substance abuse, whereas others are primary and stem from the interaction of biological predisposition with early developmental wounds and experiences (Kaufman 1994).

Music listening as an act of self-abuse

Self-abusive behavior occurs in people with borderline personality disorders, in situations of fear from pain, caused by an outside agent, as an attempt to regain control over the original trauma (Appelbaum 1996). When people inflict pain upon themselves—or listen to "painful" music— they control the situation. They are in charge of when the pain occurs and how hard it will be, as opposed to former traumas they have experienced. I cannot say whether my informants, or my clients in general, are borderline personalities, but many, for sure, are posttraumatic at some level.

In many cases, people with borderline personalities experience themselves as having no protection against invasion of the surrounding reality into their personal space; almost as if their bodies have no skin, and external stimuli seem to flood them when they experience intolerable feelings of failure and humiliation. According to Kernberg (1984) these people have no effective, available coping mechanisms for affect regulation, apart from self-abuse. When these personality traits join with the lifestyle and turmoil of drug abuse, the emotional situation can become unbearable.

Listening to music enables one to feel. Such is self-abuse—sometimes it enables one to feel something, anything, when all else is dark, cold, and lacking emotion. Many drug addicts relate that during periods of heavy use—especially of heroin—they feel like "living-dead", without feelings or human vitality. Whereas while listening to music, they feel alive and connected to their own emotional-experiential repertoire from their past and present.

Music as a drug substitute

The process of separation from the drugs is not the same for all addicts. Some report that, after going through withdrawal symptoms, they do not feel a physical yearning for the drugs they took. Their main struggle is dealing with the emotions and memories that were suppressed by the drugs, and at this stage begin to flood their consciousness. Others claim that they are unable to find emotional and physical equilibrium, experience mood swings between despair and joy, depression and excitability, and have difficulties relaxing or falling asleep. They tend to look for something that will fill the emotional and physical void they experience: coffee and cigarettes, sport, hard physical work—or music.

Clearly, music is different from the other "drug substitutes" mentioned here. It is a complex stimulus that affects many levels of its consumers' psyche. Music is an auditory stimulus with aesthetic dimensions and physiological effects. It can be relaxing or exciting; it can arouse pleasant or unpleasant memories; it enables access to otherworld realms—to fantasy or spirituality; and it is interlocked with ethnic, social, and cultural identities.

Can music replace drugs during periods of abstinence? Some of the informants related to this question. Many of them said at times that "music is like drugs" but all agreed that music's ability to affect one's mood or bodily experiences is weaker, or subtler, than that of drugs. Music touches the soul in a different, less total manner. Its effect is more gentle and in some cases more controllable than that of a chemical substance injected, inhaled, or ingested into the body and then manipulating biochemical and neurological functions. It seems that for some addicts, during periods of abstinence, music can become an alternative object to which they can cling and extract emotional and physical qualities, such as relaxation, diversion, excitement, companionship, security, and even a sense of meaning to their lives.

While listening to music with my clients, during our music therapy sessions, I am often impressed by the special quality of their attentiveness. They seem to be immersed in the music as in a total experience. Their listening appears to be a two-way process: they seem to be drawn into the music while, at the same time, trying to draw the music into themselves. It feels as if they are trying to extract to the full what the music can provide, an attempt to "squeeze out the last drops," similar to the long, last draw on a cigarette. This is a total physical and emotional experience. Many of our clients appear to have a vast need to assimilate something from the outside into their body, into their soul; a need that stems from a sensation of emptiness, of a void.

The theory of self-medication

We have seen how music listening can enable a total experience of holding, a sensory experience of being contained by something external that at the same time penetrates a person's being. The desire to listen to music can be explained by a deep longing to return and experience the primary object (Bolas 1987 in Franck-Schwebel 2002).

Let us divert, in order to become acquainted with Khantzian's theory of self-medication (1985), and we will soon see how it connects to the issues we are dealing with. This theory explains the use and abuse of certain drugs (mainly heroin and cocaine) as an attempt at self-medication for psychic pain. The pain can be traced to external events such as traumas or early deprivation, often in combination with congenital, neurological defects such as attention deficit disorder (ADD), learning disabilities, or an abnormally high or low sensory threshold. Choosing the preferred drug is not unintentional. The drug of choice is one whose pharmacological attributes can deal effectively with the personal, physical, and emotional pain the user is dealing with.

One client told me that heroin, for example, "fit me like a glove" and enabled him "to feel like a normal person". He had tried other drugs but wasn't comfortable with them. In comparison, other clients related that they tried heroin once or twice, didn't like its effects, and moved on to other drugs.

In addition to this process of adapting one's drug to one's ingrained disposition, many users aim at matching a drug to a specific, momentary emotional or physical state. Poly-drug users "play" with the drugs at their disposal, in order to achieve desired effects. It is also common to use certain drugs to reduce the negative effects of other drugs, or to relieve withdrawal symptoms of other drugs.

There seems to be a transfer of this behavior of relying on something external that will change internal states (preferably immediately) to behaviors concerning music listening and the kind of music chosen at any given time.

At face value, this seems simple and logical. In areas in which one has control, one will search for stimulation that will change one's inner state from an undesirable to a desirable one. Many of our clients seem to fluctuate between a need for equilibrium and a desire for excitation. They tend to use their music as they formally used their drugs. Music, used here as a drug substitute, is unique in the seemingly infinite variations and genres, and the moods and emotions one can derive from it. Music listening may become, during periods of abstinence, a form of self-medication.

Music listening as a substitute for social/emotional interactions

Some of my informants spoke about their preference for music that has a "human touch": a singer, lyrics, and acoustic or electronic instruments—as opposed to electronic, computerized music. They need to believe the singer, and want to think that he or she is singing about their own personal experiences, and not just "making music to make money," as one informant said.

From this yearning we can assume that this type of music has the ability to represent human interactions for the listeners. The need to believe the musicians, and the search for their touch on the instruments, exposes the listener's longing for human contact.

In contrast, other informants spoke about their preference for synthesized, computerized music (trance, techno, etc.) during their drug-abusing periods. They described these musical genres as having the power to disconnect—themselves from others, and themselves from their own inner emotions.

It seems as if the more personal genres of music, mentioned above, do connect—to human sensitivities, emotions, and vitality. Many drug addicts have a strong yearning for vital, emotional human contact, for excitement and aesthetic enjoyment, and seem to try to extract these from the music they listen to. The connection to these experiences, via the music, is possible without the listeners having to make an effort in areas that may be difficult for them—interpersonal relationships, and taking initiative and responsibility for enriching their lives with positive experiences. The music listening is a passive activity but enables significant internal, emotional work. It seems that music may function not only as a substitute for drugs, but also for external, social, and human experiences. Part of our therapeutic work is to identify this tendency and to see how these needs can be externalized into real, everyday experiences.

Rehabilitation as immigration

The changes that addicts go through during the process of treatment and rehabilitation may be compared to immigration from one country to another. Literature dealing with immigration from a psychoanalytical viewpoint outlines three stages in the emotional process of immigration (Grinberg and Grinberg 1984). These stages may, with some slight changes, be borrowed for our benefit, describing the transition from the culture of addiction to the culture of recovery (White 1996):

1. Emotional pain stemming from what was lost or left behind, fear
    of the unknown, loneliness, and helplessness. And in our interest:
    mourning for the drugs and their effects, for the relationship one had
    with the drugs and the lifestyle one has left behind; fear and feelings
    of helplessness regarding one's ability to live a drug-free life.

2. After some time, the pain of the loss subsides and fades into sorrow
    and longing; the immigrant develops an ability to bear the pain and
    recognize it. Assimilation of some components of the new culture and
    integration between inner and outer realities begin to occur.

3. Rediscovery of aspirations and plans for the future. The past gains
    realistic proportions and does not interfere with life in the present.
    Integration of the original culture with the new culture is possible
    now, without the need to concede either. Regarding our subject, this
    last process must be revised, because addicts must give up the culture
    of drug use in order to move on to the culture of recovery (White
    1996). Holding on to any components of the drug culture would
    endanger the clean addict's recovery.

As we have seen so far, the music the addicts listened to in their past,
especially during drug use, has for many of them significant cultural
meanings. The issue of giving up this music or not, as part of their recovery
process, is one of great importance for some of our clients.

Sasha, born in Russia, emigrated to Israel at the age of 20. He is an
immigrant in more than one way. He must deal with the differences between
the Russian culture he was raised in and the Israeli culture of his new home.
In addition, he must deal with the passage from the drug culture to the
culture of recovery, like all his friends in rehabilitation treatment. He spoke
about his life in the therapeutic community as a time of passage. He claimed
that he did not know the codes of acceptable conduct, and felt extremely
uncomfortable. Relating to "Russian shanson,"[1] his preferred music, he felt
split; he still listened to the music from his Russian drug-using and criminal
past, but no longer lived that lifestyle. About his former life, he said:

> It's what I was my whole life, I'm used to it, it's easy, that's where I
> feel comfortable. I know what to do there, how to behave. Here [in the
> therapeutic community] I don't know how to behave. Back there—
> everybody knows me, they'll always accept me... Today, it's like I'm
> living one kind of life and listening to music from another life... I'm
> not living like I'm used to, getting into fights and gambling...but I

---

1   Russian shanson — a local genre of popular songs whose texts depict the lives of
    criminals. The songs vary, having sentimental, romantic, tough, or humoristic contents.

listen to that music, from there…the music is from there but I'm living here.

It seems that Sasha is still immersed in the first stage, mentioned above, possibly on the verge of stage two:

I want to go back to where I used to be. But maybe by listening to those songs, and identifying with the words, I remember what happened, and how it was so hard there…maybe that helps me stay here, and not go back… The music connects me to that life, I miss it, it's hard for me to forget where I came from… I grew up with these songs, and they tell about my life.

Sasha seems here to be debating his relationship with his music, which symbolizes his connection to his past life of drug abuse, gambling, and crime: "that will always be my past…that's what I have left from my past."

Apprehension toward change

I don't recognize myself without my drugs and my music. (Addict client)

As described above, the first stage of immigration includes pain from the loss of what was left behind and fear of the unknown. Boris and Yelena both spoke about their fear and apprehension from the changes they experienced during their time in treatment, changes which also showed themselves in their music-listening habits.

Boris said:

It happened slowly, without me deciding. I found myself listening to my shanson music less and less. I'm afraid to be without it…I think… I don't believe that I'll ever be without it completely… I have to hear a song or two, every once in a while.

Boris, like Sasha, grew up with these songs. They are strongly connected with his family and hometown. He is afraid that, by unintentionally listening less and less to this music, he will lose his ties with his past and with his identity. After leaving behind his criminal behavior and drug abuse, the music is his last connection to his past and he is afraid to relinquish it. Who will he be without his music?

Yelena, a fan of Russian punk and heavy rock music, spoke about her change. She found herself listening to, and enjoying, disco and pop music:

In the heavy rock and punk, the words were about life, and significant things... I hardly listen to that anymore. When I noticed what was happening, I...was scared. You know, the first time that I felt good, that I was happy...I couldn't accept it. And I looked at all this light, stupid pop music I found myself listening to, and actually enjoying...I couldn't take it. It's not me...I was so used to bad things.

Here also we witness a gradual, unintentional process. The changes in both Boris's and Yelena's music-listening habits symbolize a much broader change in their emotional stability, behavior, and positive outlook on life.

Music listening as a high-risk factor

High-risk factors are any life situations which may endanger a recovering addict's obligation to recovery. All emotional and environmental cues and triggers that bring about memories of use or weaken one's self-efficacy, and which may bring about relapse to substance abuse, must be identified and dealt with in treatment.

In order to identify the dangers of music as a high-risk factor, four aspects must be examined:

1. music as a cognitive cue, recalling the total experience of drug use
2. identification with depressive textual contents in songs
3. music listening as an act of self-abuse—absence of symbolic distance
4. music defining criminal identity.

The relations between these aspects will be different from one addict to another. In one, the emotional aspects may be emphasized more while in another—the cognitive or cultural ones. But in all cases we must examine the interplay between these aspects in order to understand the complexity of the relationship with music and the possibility of it becoming a danger to the addict's abstinence.

Music can evoke emotional and physical responses not just because of the music's properties, but because music recreates a mental and emotional representation of the essence of the moment when it was first heard (Ortiz 1997). The memory evoked can be of negative experiences or emotions, or of actual drug use. The established links between certain types of music and the euphoric recall of drug intoxication, reinforced through thousands of repetitions, serve as powerful connections to the culture of addiction (White 1996). Nahum relates: "Even now, I can listen to Pink Floyd, and straight away it takes me to...places of chaos, drugs, grass, alcohol..."

Music, as a cue that can bring about memories of drug abuse, can also function as a warning signal before relapse. An abstaining addict going through a crisis might, unaware, find himself listening to his drug abuse-related music, which he may have stopped listening to as a result of his abstinence and changed lifestyle. The music is not the cause of his emotional upheaval but reflects it. The music may heighten his emotional unstableness. But, if he has acquired awareness of the connection between certain kinds of music and negative emotions, such as loss of control, depression, or anxiety, the actual act of listening to the music may become a warning sign, or red light—a signal to stop, evaluate his situation, and seek help.

Both Zohar and Yelena related situations in which listening to their music brought about painful and conflictual emotions and negative memories. Zohar said:

> There were times when I wasn't using but I listened to my old songs… and it was tough. In the past, the drugs used to block out some of the depressing feelings the music brought up… I try not to listen to that stuff anymore. I really want to but I know it's not good for me… It can harm me if I listen to it when I'm clean… I could go back to my drugs.

Yelena told about a time when she was working at a rehabilitation center, and met a new client who played the guitar. She asked him if he knew songs of her favorite punk group, songs that she had stopped listening to since finishing her own rehabilitation treatment:

> and he started to play a song, and we sang together, and it was bad… Suddenly I heard again all those words and I could understand them differently…and…no, no, I don't want it… I stopped singing… I felt that if I continued I would lose myself, I'd fall in love with the music again, easily, I'd find myself back in the dark, where I was before.

Here, Yelena described a situation where she found herself toying with her boundaries. She asked the client to play the music, knowing, maybe unconsciously, what it would cause her to feel. In retrospect she understood the mistake she had made and could stop it in time.

From the three transcriptions above, we can see how clean addicts understand the danger the music can have for them, and have come to the understanding that they must abstain from listening to it.

But this form of abstinence raises another problem. Heavy drug abuse, over a period of many years, may form "black holes" in the personal narrative of the addict, similar to what may occur in cases of post-trauma. It is possible that the emotional stagnation caused by the drugs—and the complete dependence upon them as an object that disables normal emotional and social development—can cause the addict to feel that his years of drug use were a lost period of his life. Many clients relate important milestones— marriage, birth of children, deaths of family members—as events, which, even though they themselves were physically present, had no emotional meaning for them.

The experience of continuity in one's personal narrative is crucial in building a strong identity. An important part of the treatment of addicts includes examining these 'black holes' found in the personal narrative, in an attempt to rebuild this lack of sense of continuity. Music has a function is this work. By being gradually exposed to music identified with different periods of the client's life, from before and during drug abuse, the addict may be able to emotionally connect to events from these times. The music can raise memories and emotions, formally blocked. This process is especially important for those clients born and raised in other countries. Their past memories are tied to people and places now disconnected from them. Listening to the music from their past can help revive memories from their childhood and youth and enables them to incorporate these memories in a comprehensive life-narrative.

For Boris and Sasha, listening to the shanson songs enables them, on one hand, to preserve some form of continuity with their past and with the memories of their families and hometowns. On the other hand, holding on to these songs may preserve their social and ethnic identity of Russian criminals, which will make their transition into the society of recovery more difficult.

Many of our clients, as we have seen, make conscious decisions to relinquish the music from their past, and so perpetuating their "black holes." During the first few years of rehabilitation, addicts may find themselves in a trap—they must activate rigid mechanisms in order to deal with their longing for drugs and the drug-abusing lifestyle. These mechanisms dictate the need to distance themselves from anything that will remind them of their past. This behavior is in opposition to the emotional need to form a continuous narrative.

Each recovering addict must solve this dilemma individually. Some of them, during the early stages of their rehabilitation, make the painful decision to stop listening to some of the music from their past. After a few years, many of them find that the music does not pose a threat for them anymore, and that they can go back to it. Interestingly, they may find that this music, which is identified with their drug abuse and criminal behavior, is no longer relevant to their new lifestyle and holds little more than nostalgic interest for them.

Music listening as a positive experience

Nahum spoke about the ways music enhances his new drug-free lifestyle:

> I hardly ever sit, nowadays, and listen to music for hours like I used to. Let's say, on the weekend, when I'm cleaning or cooking, I'll turn on the stereo, and it makes like this special atmosphere, 'cause I don't do it every day…and the sounds caress me, it's like a background…and sometimes I'll put music on so as not to hear all the…quiet around me, I don't want to think so much, don't want to feel so lonely…the quiet makes me dig inside, I don't want to go there too much.

Lehtonen quotes Racker (Racker 1951 in Lehtonen 2002) who wrote about music's ability to protect an individual against unpleasant feelings and yet, at the same time, give psychic strength to face and overcome them. Music can also be used in frightening and unpleasant situations, for instance against silence representing loneliness. Music is perceived as a social experience —even when one listens alone, there is an illusion of a supporting group (Kohut and Levarie 1990).

Dima related how he uses music:

> There are times when I get inside myself too much…it frightens me. Music lets me connect better, it's like without the music my mind goes so many different ways, I can't stay focused, I get depressed… I don't feel good when my thoughts are all messed up… Music focuses me and helps me stay on track… It's like I've turned my music into a tool that keeps me straight, helps me cope with my life without drugs.

We saw above how Frith (1987) wrote that music can help one connect to emotions while simultaneously keeping the listener at a safe distance.

Coda

I hope that the heightened understanding gained from my research will benefit therapeutic work with addicts, and cause more awareness of the importance of music and other cultural aspects in their treatment. We have seen that, for many addicts, music has a powerful destructive potential. It can be abused, as drugs are. It can be misused and lead one into a vicious circle of dependency and self-destructiveness. But music has the potential to heal. I believe that, by achieving a deeper understanding of the relationships addicts form with music, we can assist them in discovering more of their inner selves as manifested in their music. By rehabilitating their music-listening habits, they can begin to incorporate music into their lives as a source of enjoyment and enrichment.

The informants

- **Boris**: aged 27; heroin abuser. Emigrated to Israel from Russia by himself at the age of 17.
- **Dima**: aged 24; poly-drug abuser. Emigrated to Israel from Russia with his family at the age of 9.
- **Nahum**: aged 40; poly-drug plus alcohol abuser. Studied music in high school and is very talented at his instrument. Israeli born, second generation of North African immigrants.
- **Sasha**: aged 25; addicted to opium, heroin, and gambling. Emigrated to Israel from Russia by himself at the age of 20.
- **Yelena**: aged 27; poly-drug plus alcohol abuser. Emigrated to Israel from Russia with her family at the age of 10.
- **Zohar**: aged 20; drugs of choice were cannabis, ecstasy, and LSD. Israeli born, second generation of Moroccan immigrants.

Acknowledgment

This research was done with the assistance of the Israeli Anti-Drug Authority.

CHAPTER 4

The Role of Music Therapy in Helping Drug Dependants

Mohammad Reza Abdollahnejad

Introduction

In recent years, with advances in research, different rehabilitation and treatment methods have been employed to improve substance abusers' recovery. Music therapy, in this regard, is an adjunctive and adoptable modality that can play a significant role in rehabilitation (James 1988a, 1988b). On the other hand, music therapy has been welcomed substantially by substance abusers for its dynamic, open-ended creative attitude and non-threatening nature.

This chapter is about music therapy activities in a therapeutic community in Tehran that involve the use of lyric analysis and song sharing. A self-designed questionnaire is used to assess the effects of music that drug dependants listened to during their addiction period. A total of 25 sessions of lyric analysis/song sharing were held. Clients were asked about their feelings at the end of each session. Each session was recorded. Conclusions showed the use of lyric analysis and song sharing was particularly useful for enabling residents to express their feelings and thoughts. Finally, it was found that the music that drug dependants had listened to during their addiction had positively affected their relapse and aggressive consuming.

Therapists who work with substance abusers and drug dependants usually regard their clients' feelings and emotions as mysteries. Drug dependants, in accordance with their lifestyle, apply the defence mechanisms of rationalising, minimising, manipulating, denying and lying. Such defence mechanisms are the roots of not being able to recognise and express emotions and feelings (James 1988a, 1988b).

Music therapy has proved to be a most effective method in dealing with such defences. Treder-Wolff (1990b) discusses how such creative musical experiences can remove emotional conflicts and inner blocks that are known to be obstacles towards change and growth.

The treatment of addiction in Iran dates back 50 years, following a governmental ban on drug abuse, when therapeutic centres were established. At that time, medical treatment was the only modality of treatment. However, in the course of time and as other treatment methods improved, different rehabilitation methods were considered. In recent decades, various methods such as psychotherapy (individually and in groups), methadone maintenance treatment, 'twelve-step groups' and therapeutic communities emerged. Out of the aforementioned approaches, the therapeutic community is the most recent and dates back to 2001.

Music therapy is also in its early stages and the Music Application in Mental and Physical Health Association (MAMPHA) in Iran has started to research music therapy since 2001.

The research work presented here is the first experience in Iran of the application of music therapy in a therapeutic community for substance abusers and drug dependants. The objective of this research was to evaluate the effectiveness and role of some methods of music therapy such as lyric analysis and song sharing on the expression of feelings and emotions of substance abusers and drug dependants residing at Tehran Therapeutic Community. The same techniques have been successfully used and experienced in other countries.

Music Application in Mental and Physical Health Association (MAMPHA)

In 1996 a group of university students in the fields of medical sciences, psychology and music at Tehran University started their studies in music therapy. They held workshops, studied music therapy resources and conducted research based on the local culture with the assistance of university supervisors. Some of the experts who had a central role in forming a music therapy association were Dr Hassan Ashayeri, Dr Kianoosh Hashemian, Dr

Saeed Sharifian, Dr Masoud Nematian,[1] Dr Mohammad Joghataee and Dr Shiva Dolat Abadi.

In 1997, the first nationwide congress was held in Iran and, subsequent to feedback arising from this which reflected an existing need in the community, it was decided that an association had to be established with the mission of extending and developing the overall aspects of music therapy both quantitatively and qualitatively, including the training of experts.

Finally, in 2001, an association was established. Since then, the association has succeeded in holding long-term and short-term training courses and workshops, as well as creating a database as a reference for interested researchers. The association has also tried and applied music therapy in the treatment of children with mental and physical disabilities, besides substance abusers. The association has also held five nationwide congresses aimed at a wider exchange of information with researchers and experts in the field. However, the association has had some difficulties, such as finding a specific location, financial challenges, gaining recognition as a therapeutic approach and establishing a university course. Nevertheless, music therapy has a very good future with enthusiastic supporters in Iran.

Tehran Therapeutic Community

According to the National Institute on Drug Abuse (NIDA) (2005) the concept of therapeutic community for the treatment of substance abusers and drug dependants has been in use for about 40 years. In general, therapeutic communities are divided into two categories:

1. therapeutic communities for treatment of drug dependants
2. therapeutic communities for treatment of clients with mental health issues.

Therapeutic communities for treatment of drug dependants are divided into various types and we will go on to discuss the model that we use at Tehran Therapeutic Community.

> The Therapeutic Communities can be distinguished from other major drug treatment modalities in two fundamental ways. First, the Therapeutic Communities offer a systematic treatment approach that is guided by an explicit perspective on the *drug use disorder, the person, recovery, and right living.* Second, the primary therapist and teacher in

---

1   Dr Nematian sadly passed away in 2007. He and I were founders of the first music therapy association in Iran. He had a leading role in founding, developing and expanding music therapy in Iran.

> the Therapeutic Communities is the *community* itself, which consists of
> the social environment, peers, and staff members who, as role models
> of successful personal change, serve as guides in the recovery process.
> (De Leon 1994, p.18; emphasis in original)

Many individuals admitted to therapeutic communities have a history of
social functioning, education/vocational skills, and positive community
and family ties that have been eroded by their substance abuse. For these
people, recovery involves rehabilitation – relearning or re-establishing
healthy functioning, skills and values, as well as regaining physical and
emotional health. Other therapeutic communities' residents have never
acquired functional lifestyles. For these people, the therapeutic communities
are usually their first exposure to orderly living. Recovery, for them, involves
rehabilitation, learning behavioural skills for the first time, examining
attitudes, and promoting values associated with socialised living (NIDA
2005).

In addition to the importance of the community as a primary agent
of change, a second fundamental therapeutic communities' principle
is 'self-help'. Self-help implies that the individuals in treatment are the
main contributors to the change process. 'Mutual self-help' means that
individuals also assume partial responsibility for the recovery of their peers,
an important aspect of an individual's own treatment (NIDA 2005).

> The aims of treatment are global in the Therapeutic Communities.
> The primary psychological goal is to change the negative patterns of
> behaviour, thinking and feeling that predispose drug use; the main
> social goal is to develop a responsible, drug-free lifestyle. Stable
> recovery, however, depends on a successful integration of these social
> and psychological goals. Behavioural change is unstable without
> insight, and insight is insufficient without experience. Thus, conduct,
> emotions, skills, attitudes, and values must be integrated to ensure
> enduring lifestyle changes and a positive personal social identity. The
> social and psychological goals of the Therapeutic Communities shape
> its treatment regime as well as defining several broad assumptions
> concerning its view of recovery. (De Leon 1994, p.21)

The Tehran Therapeutic Community is a drug-free concept-based residential
therapeutic community that uses a staged and hierarchical model in which
treatment stages are related to increased levels of individual and social
responsibility. The sense of a strong, structured hierarchical environment in
which all participants and staff have specific tasks, responsibilities and rights
is crucial to the success of most therapeutic community programmes (Mello

et al. 1997). It was established in 2000. In the centre, substance abusers and drug dependants are admitted following a detoxification process, an initial interview and assessment by social workers, as well as psychologists collating a drug-use history, family background and using the Addiction Severity Index (McLellan *et al.* 1980).

Subsequent to admission, clients have to go through four phases of treatment:

1. **Orientation phase** where the programme plus rules, regulations and philosophy of the therapeutic community are introduced to the client. The client can decide during this phase whether or not they can complete the whole process. Visits by family members are not allowed in this phase. This phase lasts approximately one month.

2. **Treatment phase**, which lasts for three months, where the client uses several therapeutic programmes that include attending all therapeutic community meetings, therapeutic groups, training and counselling that are available at the centre. Unlike the first phase, family visits are permitted.

3. **Re-entry phase** where the client is gradually released from the centre in the course of a two-month period. The objectives of this phase are to give clients, step by step, a chance to become familiar with the environment outside the centre and to put into practice all the lessons learned in the therapeutic community in the real world. In addition, it is an opportunity for them to exchange their experiences gained outside the centre with other residents. They have the opportunity to talk with therapists about problems they face and find ways of solving them.

4. **Follow-up phase** where the clients attend the weekly group therapy sessions held at the centre and the social workers follow up on the status of the client, by phone or visiting the client at their place of residence.

In the first six months of therapy, the clients attend different therapeutic interventions such as group therapy, counselling, occupational therapy, training classes, vocational rehabilitation and music therapy conducted by social workers, psychologists and trained clients who have graduated from therapeutic communities.

Music therapy programme

One of the challenges of working in therapeutic communities and outpatient centres with drug dependants and substance abusers is the difficulty that clients have in expressing their feelings and thoughts in therapeutic programmes such as counselling sessions, therapeutic groups and meetings. In Tehran, the therapeutic community therapists were always faced with clients who were reluctant to express their feelings, thoughts and problems. Hence, a difficulty in assessing progress on the road to recovery was very slow.

Furthermore, these clients also had problems in communication with other residents in the therapeutic community. For instance, in sports or other recreational activities they usually stayed away from other residents and preferred to be alone and kill time. Hence, their connections with the therapeutic community at large were tenuous, which meant they became preoccupied with leaving and terminated treatment.

Because of this reluctance of clients to engage in emotional self-expression, we started the Tehran Therapeutic Community based on activities, practices and researches from around the world which demonstrated the effectiveness of music therapy in helping drug abusers to express their feelings and thoughts (James 1988a, 1988b; Treder-Wolff 1990b). As music therapy in the therapeutic community was a pioneering experience, it was necessary that the therapists and the people in charge were informed of the aims and benefits of music therapy. The briefing took place in one session. Then, in line with a planned schedule with the therapists, the clients who had difficulty in expressing their thoughts and feelings were referred to music therapy sessions.

Client details and music preferences

There were a total of 20 participants who had a history of between 5 and 15 years of substance abuse or drug dependency. Eighty per cent of the participants had heroin injection abuse and the remaining 20 per cent were addicted to opium and narcotics (see Table 4.1). The participants were all male in an age range of 22 to 50 years. Another point to note is that 60 per cent had been homeless from two to five years. Eighty per cent of the participants were sentenced to prison on charges of drug smuggling, substance abuse, robbery and fighting. In the course of 25 sessions, seven clients left the therapeutic community.

All clients took part in the programme eagerly and voluntarily because music therapy was interesting for all of the Tehran Therapeutic Community's clients, even though they were not usually so interested in engaging in therapeutic programmes. However, most of the clients were keen to be involved in the music therapy sessions. Those who weren't in the music therapy programme were very intrigued to know about it. After each session they curiously asked questions to clients who attended the programme.

Music therapy sessions

The first two sessions were allocated to familiarising the group members with the aims and benefits of the programme.

At the beginning of the first session of therapy, the clients were given a self-designed questionnaire covering the areas below.

Questions

1. their favourite music and singer (see Table 4.2)
2. type of drug they were addicted to, duration of their jail sentence (see Table 4.3) and duration of their addiction (see Table 4.4)
3. the relationship between their favourite music and actively resuming abuse.

Results

QUESTION 1

The majority of clients were fans of singers that sing sad music. They mentioned that they liked to listen to this kind of music while alone.

QUESTION 2

For duration of their jail sentence, most clients were in jail between 0 and 3 years. They were arrested by police for robbery, burglary, theft, shoplifting, fraud, carjacking or drug trafficking.

According to duration of their dependency, most of the clients had a dependency between 5 and 15 years. Furthermore, during this time most of them started their drug dependency with marihuana and alcohol and ended up with opium and especially heroin. On the other hand, most of the clients with a long history of drug dependency had a history of jail sentences for drug trafficking, burglary and so on. However, five of them had a rich family or financial support which prevented them behaving illegally to get their drug.

Table 4.1 Type of drug use

Type of drug dependency	Heroin	Alcohol	Opium	Cannabis	Narcotics	Total
Participants	16	0	3	0	1	20

Table 4.2 Favourite song and frequency of use

Favourite song	Lively (happy) music	Calm (light) music	Sad music	Total
Participants	6	3	11	20

Table 4.3 Duration of jail sentence

Duration of jail sentence/year	None	0–1	1–3	3–5	5–7	More than 7	Total
Participants	5	8	5	1	1	0	20

Table 4.4 Duration of dependency to drug

Duration of dependency to drug in years	1–5	5–10	10–15	Above 15	Total
Participants	1	9	8	2	20

QUESTION 3

The narratives told by clients while answering this third question demonstrated that the music that substance abusers listened to during their addiction period also tempted them significantly to go back to drugs during their recovery period (see also Horesh 2006a). Twelve clients mentioned that listening to some pieces of music motivated them to abuse aggressively, and eight individuals said that it didn't have any effect on them. The majority of clients, who said that music had affected them, referred to listening to songs of singers of sad music and, whenever they listened, they were motivated to abuse drugs. In fact, this kind of music encouraged them to relive their drug-use memories, especially their pleasurable time while they were using drugs.

Each session lasted for 45 to 60 minutes, and at the end of each session the clients were asked about their opinion of the therapy. Also, all sessions were videotaped and the remarks of the clients were analysed. The songs were chosen by the therapist for lyric analysis on the basis of the clients' problems, and the clients themselves chose the songs for song sharing. After each session, I discussed with the therapists the matters the clients had revealed about their ongoing feelings, and about their thoughts for solving their psychological and family problems. These discussions suggested that the clients used the music and words of the lyric analysis and song-sharing sessions to indirectly express their thoughts and feelings (see also Hedigan 2005).

Lyric analysis

In one of the lyric analysis sessions, a song named 'Niloofaraneh' by an Iranian traditional singer was used. The content of the lyric is about a person who claims to be a lover of Almighty God and requests God Almighty to become closer to him and that He makes His love to His subjects known to them all and frees them from all worldly kinds of love.

Following the playing of the recorded music, some questions were posed to the group members as follows:

- 'What the song was all about' was one of the questions to which one of the members replied that the song was about human love for their creator as opposed to other types of love; that is to say, love of wealth, worldly possessions and power. Another member considered the song to be about a desperate type who might be 'well to do' but feels nothing and that's why he seeks protection from his superior. One other member believed the lyric to be about longing and nostalgia addressed to Almighty God, who is supposed to be all knowing about human feelings and thoughts. Finally, another member stated the song was about a person who feels guilty and requests forgiveness for all of his bad behaviours.

- 'Put yourselves in the shoes of the singer and guess how the singer had been feeling' was another question asked of the group participants. One member replied that the singer had been feeling unsatisfied about all things and looked at God as the solution to this problem. Another one pointed out that nobody recognised the singer and so the singer had turned to God. One other member considered that the singer was very pessimistic about his future and nobody could help him because of his loneliness and that everything and everybody was against him.

- 'How and what you feel towards Almighty God' was a third question asked. One group member said that he felt God never heard his voice and that there was no contact between him and the creator. Another member stated Almighty God never forgave him because he had behaved disgracefully towards everybody, including his parents. A remark by another group member was that he loved God but disliked himself because whenever he had a problem he remembered God!

In another lyric analysis session, we selected a song by an Iranian pop singer. The song name was 'Doll'. The song was sad and the content of the song was about someone who is in love with a pretty girl and after a while realises that she has no feelings for him. It is as if he has loved a doll all the while.

In this lyric, we picked some questions to extract the thoughts of the group about the song. The first question was posed about what the subject of the song was. One of the members said thoughtfully that the song wasabout a person who has been pursuing a goal without achieving it, and now feels his time has gone to waste and that he has left no door open behind him to be able to go back! Another member considered it was about a person looking for water in the desert who knows that he cannot find it. His action is futile but, even so, he still is looking for water. One other member stated that the song was about a 'dull thing', like all of us have in our life, such as drugs, girlfriends, power and money, and all of those things that make us forget our true selves and think about something else, although we all know that we are making mistakes and forgetting our ultimate goal. Despite this knowledge, we continue in our futility.

One other question asked was what the singer was complaining about. In reply, one member said that the singer was complaining about himself because he had been pursuing an untrue love and was upset because he didn't realise the fact about his love earlier. Another member said the singer was angry because he thought he would have a pleasurable time with his 'doll thing' and couldn't understand that there was no future with a doll and a doll is not a person to rely on. Another member of the group replied that the singer was complaining about his bad luck. If he had good luck, he wouldn't be faced with this girl and could continue his life normally. When asked to solve the problem of the singer, the group members replied that the singer must refer to himself and get his needs right, be hopeful about the future, and start a new life.

Song sharing

In one of the song-listening sessions a group member selected a song with the title 'Tak' by an Iranian pop singer. The song was about a period of the singer's life that reminded the group member of his own past. He said in a sad tone that he was born and brought up in a poor family and that he has always felt inferior when going out with his friend, who enjoyed a rich and educated upbringing. In addition, he suffered from a handicapped leg that further contributed to him having a low opinion of himself and inability to deal with the opposite sex. In the same phase of his life, he made friends with a cannabis consumer. While consuming cannabis, he felt happy and relieved. This trend continued till he ended up consuming heroin.

The group started analysing his situation and the causes of his addiction to drugs and asked him what caused him to start with drugs. He said that his family neglected him and considered him less confident and efficient compared to his brother. His brother got all the family attention and care. One group member suggested that he was seeking the attention and confirmation of others in all that he did and was following the same practice even now that he was a resident at the therapeutic community.

He replied that his friend had nicknamed him a 'free-loader' because of his financial limitations. Therefore he performed menial tasks like car washing and house cleaning to compensate. He further explained the cold relationship between his parents. When asked if he tried to have a girlfriend, despite all his problems and shortcomings, he said that at the beginning of his drug abuse he fell in love with a girl whom he did not succeed in marrying, as her family objected to the marriage because he was handicapped. It could also be that the girl's family had learned about his addiction. Despite the girl marrying someone else, they are still in love and have a romantic relationship.

On another song-sharing session, one of the group members chose a song about 'Mother'. The content of the song was about a person who had lost his mother and felt lonely without her presence. He continually revives his mother's stories and her advice. The member who chose this song explained his own story. While he was crying, he stated that when he and his brother were under the influence of drugs they had hit their mother and stolen things from her room. On one occasion they even thought of killing her. His mother died last year and he felt guilty. He could not even participate in her funeral ceremony. Until her death, his mother continually expressed a wish to see him, despite his awful behaviour towards her. He revealed that several times he attempted suicide but each time he accidentally survived. He also stated that he was ambivalent towards continuing his treatment and leaving the therapeutic community. The only thing that caused him to stay in the therapeutic community was his mother's demand that he stay clean of drugs.

Findings

The use of music therapy in the therapeutic community was a useful experience in working with substance abusers. The clients who participated in this programme expressed their feelings, thoughts and especially their intimate stories. Some of these were secrets that had been concealed for many years, but during music therapy sessions many of these feelings, thoughts and secrets could be disclosed. For instance, one of the clients who talked in a song-sharing session had resided in the therapeutic community for about three months. During his stay, in most of the other meetings, group therapies and counselling sessions, he was silent. Therefore, when he talked during his song-sharing session about his life and problems, he surprised the other group members.

Clients who attended the music therapy programme started to communicate easier with other clients in the group or community. They engaged actively in meetings and groups and hence they could share their pain and history with other people. They progressed in treatment and asked for help from residents and therapists in solving problems. Actively seeking help was a strategy that they had not considered before.

Clients used music and words as a vehicle to express their problems and secrets. They disclosed their feelings without fear and shared them with other group members. They exchanged their experience in the groups and discussed this with each other. It was an opportunity for them to know more about each other and benefit from each member's experience.

An additional observation we made during this study was that the music to which drug dependants listened during their former addiction also promoted cravings during recovery. Some music that clients listen to during their drug use revives the atmosphere of that time and hence can jeopardise their recovery. This is an example of state-dependent learning where specific memories and emotional states are related to the physiological and mental state of the person. People in an intoxicated state only remember when they are intoxicated, not when they are sober. To recall those memories, it is important to become intoxicated again.

Discussion

In the course of the 25 sessions of lyric analysis and song sharing, the participants discussed deep existential issues that were not discussed in other types of therapy sessions. The participants expressed their feelings and thoughts more freely and openly without any holding back. These feelings and thoughts included forbidden love affairs and private, previously undiscussed issues with their families or close friends.

The participants also took an active part in discussions that engaged others in expressing opinions and experiences. We noted a close interaction between group members that resulted in a mutual learning about each other's difficulties and feelings, and also in being responsible and committed to solving each other's problems. We believe that this mutuality plays an important role in recovery. At the end, the participants proved highly interested and motivated and they insisted we continue. As a consequence, I increased the duration of the discussions.

To conclude, I would like to mention that despite the complexity of the participants' issues and problems in expressing feelings and thoughts, and their habitual reluctance to participate in group therapies and counselling, music therapy proved to be one of the most preferred therapeutic interventions at the Tehran Therapeutic Community.

CHAPTER 5

'How to Deal Music'? Music Therapy with Clients Suffering from Addiction Problems: Enhancing Coping Strategies

Irene T.F. Dijkstra and Laurien G. Hakvoort

This chapter is a revised version of I. Dijkstra and L. Hakvoort (2004) 'How to deal music? Enhancing coping strategies in music therapy with clients suffering from addiction problems.' *Music Therapy Today V* (online), November. Available at www.musictherapytoday.net.

Introduction

This chapter describes a music therapeutic technique that the authors use in their daily practice as music therapists with clients suffering from addiction problems. After explaining the theoretical backgrounds, this chapter offers a music therapy methodology. Musical assignments stress the added value of action-oriented methods of music therapy combined with verbal processing which aim to enhance coping strategies of clients.

Clients suffering from addiction are commonly known to encounter major setbacks and problems during the treatment processes and thereafter. Simply by listening to 'Brown Sugar' by the Rolling Stones or techno-house music, some clients already start craving for heroine or XTC (ecstasy). Yet, music can also be used in a therapeutic way to help clients with substance dependencies to combat their addiction.

This chapter describes a music therapy programme specifically tailored to treat clients with addiction problems, which aims to tackle some of the major difficulties and specific impairments of these clients. The authors depart from the biopsychosocial model in the treatment of addictions. The focus of the music therapy programme is behavioural, intertwined with a cognitive-psychotherapeutic approach. The goal of the programme is to offer a client insight into his[1] behaviour and alternative ways to make changes in his reactions. Music is used as a powerful tool to encourage people to act (Hakvoort 2002) and show their coping strategies, without being aware of doing so. Music therapy addresses the underlying psychological and social problems of addiction. Music touches on feelings of longing, or even craving, as well as pain and pleasure. The focus of this chapter will be on how the programme enhances coping strategies of clients with addiction problems.

This chapter makes use of different terms for addiction, partly to distinguish between different stages of consumption (use, abuse, dependency, addiction), and partly to avoid using the term 'addiction' too often. To describe addictive substances (excluding cigarettes) the term 'psychoactive substances' is used, in order to underscore their influence on the psychological perception and reaction of their consumers.

Addiction

The use of psychoactive substances is widespread. Use of these substances can proceed to abuse and might turn into dependency or addiction. The way an addiction evolves is a multifaceted process, which varies in time and across people, influenced by biological dispositions, psychological factors and social attitudes. For a long time, a major division existed between people who abused alcohol and those who used narcotics. A more recent phenomenon is so-called 'poly-drug abuse'. People use stimulating narcotics ('ice', cocaine) and alternate them with downers (heroin, benzodiazepine). One of the latest 'trends' in addiction is the combined use of alcohol and party drugs (such as XTC), especially by young people.

De Jong (2006) describes the downfall from the use of psychoactive substances, to their abuse, dependency and eventual addiction. It is evident

---

1   In this chapter the authors choose to use the masculine form. He, him, his or man can also be read as she, her and woman.

that no gradual progression in between these phases exists. Somewhere in the process an abrupt changing point of no return occurs. At that moment, people lose their control over the use of psychoactive substances. The person experiences a disturbed order in stimuli, which leads him to suddenly focus his memory towards substance use. The craving for substances appears sooner and sooner, and the person's ability to control his behaviour towards abuse declines. De Jong suggests that these are complex processes, which take place in the brain. Hence, he refers to addiction as a chronic brain disease. The Dutch Health Care Council (2002) even reports that addiction is a chronic illness of biopsychosocial aetiology.

According to O'Brien (2008) psychoactive substances change the concentrations of neurotransmitters in the long run and perhaps even permanently. All psychoactive substances affect the dopamine system, although the way in which they do differs between substances and people. Whether a person gets addicted depends on three major factors: the psychoactive substance, the user and his environment. In addition, psychoactive substances have more (side) effects as well, rewarding or damaging the addicted person. All these changes seem to bring about changes in the reward system of addicted people. Thus, O'Brien states that the disturbed reward system of clients suffering from addiction must be renewed with other stimuli. These other stimuli can change the motivation system of addicted clients as well.

Because addiction is a very complex problem, one single treatment intervention can never yield any lasting result. Most modern views about the treatment of people who suffer from substance abuse are based on the idea that treatment is only helpful if the treatment team has explicit knowledge of the client's physical conditions, his psychiatric and personality disorders, his life story, as well as his personal and social functioning. If addiction is a progressive pattern of biological, psychological, mental, behavioural and social downfall, then it can only be tackled through a multidisciplinary treatment. This requires an integration of social, cognitive and behavioural approaches, combined with medical and psychiatric treatment.

In 1979, van Dijk published a model which describes addiction as the result of a vicious circle of biological, psychological and social processes. Engel (1980) refined this model into the biopsychosocial model, which integrates multidimensional models derived from different aetiological theories. The biopsychosocial model is so attractive because not only does it approach the problem of addiction from different diagnostic angles, but it also offers opportunities to use the interrelatedness of biological, psychological and social contexts for treatment. The biopsychosocial model offers a framework to organise possible treatment interventions for clients with problems related to substance abuse. The biopsychosocial model offers a strong underpinning to multidisciplinary treatment of these clients. Music therapy is one of the modalities in the multidisciplinary treatment of this complex illness.

In this chapter, the term coping refers to the manner in which a person reacts – behaviourally, cognitively as well as emotionally – with stress-enhancing circumstances that demand adjustment (e.g. Folkman and Lazarus 1984). Each individual reacts differently if he has to cope with problematic events. How the person reacts depends upon his personality and the gravity of the problematic situation. Each person copes in his own unique way with stressful conditions. There are many factors that could contribute to the manifestation of addiction-related problematic situations. An important factor is the unique way in which an individual person observes situations, interprets them and reacts to them. This judgement determines whether a situation is interpreted as being more or less stressful. After the judgement follows a reaction, which is called the coping behaviour.

The Utrecht Coping List (Schreurs *et al.* 1993) classifies coping behaviour in four major categories:

1. situation-oriented behaviour (confrontation, evasiveness, no action, changing the problematic situation)
2. perception-influencing behaviour (optimism, accepting, compliance, pessimism, denial, devastation, changing one's reaction by influencing observation and interpretation)
3. discomfort-reducing behaviour (eliminating or diminishing uncomfortable feelings, for example by using substances such as narcotics and alcohol)
4. expression of emotions.

The effectiveness of a coping reaction is determined by the specific situation. It is impossible therefore to set one uniform standard for the effectiveness of a coping reaction. In other words, adequate coping reactions are situation-related and depend on the characteristics of the situation and on the stress the situation evokes. Thus, an adequate coping strategy for one situation at one moment could be hopelessly unsuccessful in another situation. Nevertheless, there are clearly inadequate coping strategies, especially linked with fixation in only one coping strategy such as avoidance or pessimism. The reason that these coping strategies are inadequate is because they lure a person into a negative spiral of subsequent stressful situations.

The use of psychoactive substances is not related to a specific coping behaviour. For example, the use of psychoactive substances can be a coping behaviour for reducing anxiety, to express emotions or to influence the perception of reality. One person may use psychoactive substances to encourage himself towards situation-oriented behaviour (e.g. to confront a situation). Another person might use drugs to be more able to express his feelings, or to accept an 'irreversible' situation. In any case, being 'stoned' increases feelings of inadequacy, and increasingly undermines feelings of control and self-respect.

If a person applies similar coping strategies in different situations, this is called a coping style. If a person always uses this coping style in markedly differing situations, the coping style is described as rigid. More characteristically, people suffering from addiction depend on quite restricted and rigid coping strategies. These restricted and rigid coping strategies constrain their interpersonal relationships (De Jong *et al.* 1993; Verheul 1997, Verheul, van der Bosch and Ball 2005). The addiction itself, and the negative influence of the addiction on behaviour, are affected by these deficiencies in coping strategies. Thus, the inability to apply adequate coping strategies seems to be an important trigger and risk factor for substance abusers (Dijkstra and De Jong 2003). Clients show improvement only if they are able to further develop their behavioural coping repertoire, which enhances feelings of self-esteem, self-respect and satisfaction.

Music therapy and addiction

Music therapy and addiction treatment in literature

In the treatment of clients who suffer from psychoactive substance abuse, music therapy is applied with various intervention techniques for different goals. A brief overview of recent publications on this topic provides some background to these different methods (Dijkstra and Hakvoort 2006).

Punkanen (2006b) and Erkkilä (2003) depart from a psychoanalytic approach. Both report that many clients who suffer from addiction also suffer from previous traumatisation. According to Punkanen, addiction is related to the oppression of painful experiences. Both Punkanen and Erkkilä apply a physioacoustic music therapy method. Clients are placed in a chair that vibrates in certain physical areas using sound frequencies. The vibrations aim to recall traumatic events in the client by provoking physiological reactions. They further embed their techniques in psychotherapeutic trauma treatment, guided imagery, music listening and verbal counselling. Winkelman (2003) also focuses on trauma-processing to treat clients suffering from addiction, using drum circles.

Horesh (2006a) describes a 'cue exposure' method for music therapy. Her assumption is that some musical styles provoke the same stimulus as certain substances, because clients listened to this music while using substances. She offers the clients a safe environment to experiment with the music they used during substance abuse, to raise awareness about this link. Subsequently, she lets them experiment with alternative music and forms of active musical expression to express upcoming emotions. She then uses the neurological effects of that music to motivate clients to block a triggering of the old neurological paths.

Dijkstra and De Jong (2003) describe the role of music therapy using an interpersonal behaviour model within a therapeutic community for the treatment of people who suffer from addiction. The premise of this treatment programme is that clients have major difficulties in acting flexibly and adequately in social interactions because their personal behavioural reactions are limited, rigid and inflexible. These clients tried to meet the requirements of social interaction by using psychoactive substances. Within the interpersonal behaviour model, music therapy is one of the treatment modalities. Music therapy explores the inter- and intrapersonal behaviour of a client and subsequently helps clients to extend their coping skills. Ghetti (2004) describes a music therapy method as part of a 'care' method. This method focuses on limiting the noxious consequences of substance abuse for the client and his social environment. The goal of this method is no longer abstinence, but a stabilisation of substance use.

Music therapy and addiction treatment in research

Some music therapy treatment programmes can be based directly on the results of more general research. Research by Stefano *et al.* (2004) showed that relaxation music influenced the level of natural opiates in human blood. They compared two groups of people, one group that listened to relaxation music and another group that listened to white noise (which is sound created by a random signal). They compared blood samples, and found some indications that natural morphine levels rose, and blood pressure dropped, for the subjects in the music-listening condition.

Research by Garrett *et al.* (1997) suggested that lack of motivation is one of the major pitfalls during addiction treatment. Music therapy treatment has the advantage of being a non-verbal treatment modality, which seems to preserve the motivation of most clients even during intense moments of confrontation. Horesh (2006a) describes in a qualitative research study the different dangers of using music as a treatment modality for people suffering from addiction. Music can be a cue for craving. Music often referred to by clients as triggering such emotions are heavy metal, rap, rave, techno, house and cultural ballads.

Research by Hammer (1996) and Skaggs (1997) suggested that guided imagery and music (GIM) have a positive influence on the decrease of self-perceived stress and anxiety levels of clients with addiction problems. Ward (1996) reports that music therapy strengthened self-esteem among female prisoners suffering from addiction problems and that it enabled them to increase their attention span.

Jones (2005) and Silverman (2003) reported in a literature review and a pilot study that music therapy significantly contributed to treatment motivation for poly-drug abusers. Research by Jones showed that, already after one session of song writing and text analysis during music therapy, feelings of acceptance and joy were stimulated and feelings of anxiety decreased. Silverman's quantitative study among women in long-term treatment for addiction problems compared the appreciation of music therapy with other treatment disciplines. Music therapy was highly valued as pleasant, and qualified as highly therapeutic. Music therapy was deemed especially supportive with certain treatment issues, such as diminishing impulsivity, regaining energy and relaxation.

Keen (2004) reported that music reduced resistance among adolescents suffering from addiction. During music therapy they proved to be able to learn to express their anger and anxiety in a socially acceptable manner. In addition, they developed a growing self-awareness, self-confidence and self-image during the music therapy treatment.

Music therapy and coping strategies

Gallagher and Steele (2002) made an inventory of the possible goals in the music therapeutic treatment of clients who abuse substances. This chapter focuses only on one of these goals: the enhancement of coping strategies. Music therapy offers important possibilities to improve and develop coping strategies. Music therapy is well suited to address the motivational, social and psychological components of addiction disorders. Music affects the neurological system (e.g. Stefano et al. 2004; Thaut, Nickel and Hömberg 2004), it triggers motivation (Jones 2005; Silverman 2003) and is, by virtue of its action-oriented nature, the ideal experimental setting to practise coping, interaction, communication and the expression of emotions. Playing music forces clients to act. In the action many of their coping styles become visible and audible.

If a client is able to get a cognitive hold on coping strategies, he might be willing to experiment with alternative strategies. Musical assignments given to clients are supposed to affect client behaviour through the principle of analogy (Smeijsters 2005). The principle of analogy is that musical behaviour shows major similarities with personal behaviour. The analogy process theory, as described by Smeijsters, assumes that actions performed by a person during a specific musical situation mirror the acts of this person in similar situations in their daily life. Thus, musical behaviour can be compared with non-musical behaviour.

The therapist should encourage a client to use different coping strategies by offering different musical assignments and situations. If certain behaviours occur repeatedly during these changing musical assignments, the client probably uses specific, rigid coping styles. The treatment will be directed accordingly towards an enhancement of his coping strategies, through music therapy.

A music therapy programme to enhance coping behaviour

This section presents the music therapy programme to enhance coping behaviour in clients who suffer from substance abuse. A major focus of this programme is to raise clients' awareness about the existence of alternative coping strategies. A first step in the programme is that both therapist and client become aware of the coping strategies the client uses. Substance abuse is an obvious candidate. As a coping strategy, it is usually linked to other (rigid) coping styles. Hence, the first sessions of the programme enable the music therapist to observe a client and assess his coping strategies and coping style. These sessions should also provide the client with an opportunity to get acquainted with music therapy, the therapist and possible group members. As soon as a working relationship is established, the therapist can start helping the client to relate his musical (coping) behaviour to his coping behaviour in daily situations. Often, the first sessions are held in a group setting, which increases clients' awareness that they all share the same experiences.

Clients suffering from addiction tend to cling to coping strategies like evasiveness and denial. If a music therapist were to use a one-dimensional treatment strategy, he would never be able to tackle the many biopsychosocial problems that a client encounters. Therefore, an eclectic music therapy method is applied, focusing on music, coping behaviour, action-oriented behaviour and a cognitive understanding within the biopsychosocial approach. Such an approach can be very confronting for a client. However, because music itself is often an appealing factor, clients' motivation remains high, as shown in Garrett et al. (1997), Jones (2005) and Silverman (2003). The music therapy programme is organised in five different stages.

Stage 1 – introduction

The goal of this stage in the music therapy programme is to get to know one another and to create the proper treatment conditions. This stage requires one or two sessions. Usually, the music therapist uses music listening assignments in order to find out what musical style or which songs trigger what kind of memories or reactions in the client, for example craving, avoiding, denial. Meanwhile, the music therapist assesses the client's musical history and treatment record, and determines the client's ability to function in a group.

During the first stage each client brings in his own music, and all clients listen together to their music. In this way, the programme guarantees that clients experience a 'safe' introduction, with music as an intermediate for therapeutic goals. In addition, the therapist encourages clients to verbally exchange and discuss their experiences and emotions about their music, so that they get to know each other.

The first impressions offer the therapist the opportunity to check whether a client is able to listen, and whether a client is able emotionally to assess music in a richer, more multidimensional way than the restricted judgement of beautiful versus awful. At an individual level, clients increase their awareness about the effects of music on their emotions and feelings. At a social level, the group setting offers clients the opportunity to take the step of learning to respect each other's different musical tastes. As such, the first stage provides the therapist with a first check on the client's tolerance potential.

Stage 2 – observation and assessment

The goal of this stage in the music therapy programme is to assess the client's most important coping strategies, and the client's rigidity therein, using structured rhythmic assignments for a group of clients. During all assignments, the music therapist carefully assesses any reaction of the client that occurs. Such reactions reflect problems or potential within areas such as impressibility, the flexibility in structuring situations or the ability to set boundaries. The therapist should take care that the music makes a non-threatening impression on the client, in order to maintain or stimulate the client's motivation. The group assignments that are used to assess coping strategies are rhythmic, drum-circle assignments:

1. Each client and the music therapist choose a drum. Each client plays one beat, one after the other, and together they should create a steady pulse. The therapist brings the music to a close. The purpose is to assess listening skills, anticipation skills and feeling for the music.

2.   Subsequently, the tempo or volume of the pulse is raised or lowered. The therapist brings the music to a close. The purpose of this assignment is to assess listening skills, anticipation skills, musical feeling and motor skills.

3.   The music therapist then announces to the group that the pulse has to continue, but that each group member can withdraw from playing by raising his hand. His neighbours have to continue playing their own single beat, but now earlier. The therapist brings the music to a close. The purpose of this assignment is to assess social awareness, attention span, empathetic behaviour and anticipation skills.

4.   Instead of one single beat, a small, limited pattern of beats can be repeated by the group. Each client must start at least once with a pattern of beats. They must play a rhythm which they expect all the others are able to remember and repeat. The one who started stops first. The clients stop in turn. The purpose of this assignment is to assess social awareness, attention span, empathetic behaviour, anticipation skills and individual cognitive strategies to start a pattern or remember a pattern.

5.   One client starts with his own drumming pattern. The next client joins in with his own drumming pattern, which must fit within the first pattern. Subsequently, other clients join in, one after another, with their own rhythms. The one who started stops first and then the others follow, one after the other. Clients have to take turns. In this exercise there is an explicit invitation and assessment of interactions. The purpose of this assignment is to assess social awareness, attention span, empathetic behaviour, anticipation skills, individual cognitive strategies to make up a pattern and strategies to stick to one's own pattern.

The next step incorporates assignments that aim to stimulate group cohesion:

6.   Clients play together exactly the same basic rhythm. Once the rhythm is synchronised the group has to continue to play the rhythmic pattern, and the exercise is to vary the dynamic within the whole group at the same time.

7.   Subsequently, each client is asked to play a solo, while the group plays a basic rhythmic pattern to give the solo musical grounding. Each member of the group must play his solo, can take his own time, and is invited to make variations in dynamics, pattern and tempo.

8. Finally, all group members start with one basic rhythmic pattern. They are asked to play a solo if and when they like, sometimes involving more clients at the same time.

Follow-up assignments include:

9. As above under (5), but now clients have to come to an end by themselves, without the interference of the music therapist. One client is assigned as the 'conductor' of this closure. All clients have a turn as a conductor. The purpose of this assignment is to assess social awareness, the potential to ask for attention, empathetic behaviour, anticipation skills and individual cognitive and behavioural strategies to end a situation.

10. As above under (9), but now the group has no assigned conductor. The purpose of this assignment is to assess social awareness, the potential to ask for attention, empathetic behaviour, anticipation skills and individual cognitive and behavioural strategies to end a situation.

During the second stage, the therapist assists clients in setting up a coping strategy scheme. Client reactions to assignments are observed, videotaped, analysed and discussed between the therapist and client(s). This feedback is crucial to stimulating the clients to link these insights to situations in their daily life – thus creating the analogy between musical situations and the problems they encounter in their daily life.

EXAMPLE OF STAGE 2 – OBSERVATION AND ASSESSMENT

Four men participate in the second session of the music therapy programme. They start off slightly nervous. During the first musical assignment of the drum circle, a number of situation-oriented coping mechanisms pop up. The men hardly listen to one another, and each man plays as loud as possible. Yet, they do not dare to confront each other with any inconvenience, such as the enormous noise they produce as a group.

One of the group members, Mr C, is playing very dominantly. He is a strong man, and plays extremely loud, using all the power of his muscular arms. Mr C is hardly able to listen to other people. He ridicules the group members who are less musically talented, and keeps on playing when one of the group members, or even the music therapist, is talking. He appears to be completely incapable of integrating any of the music of his peers, or even that of the therapist, into his music. Clearly, his coping style during this session is to overpower others, to diminish any discomfort by laughing about other group members, and to change his perception of the music therapy situation by becoming very sarcastic.

By contrast, Mr E plays very hesitantly, but he joins in the laughter about other group members. He has some trouble following the musical patterns and starts asking about the necessity of music therapy. But, he accepts the explanations given and continues participating in the group. When, however, *he* becomes the laughing-stock, he lays back in his chair and pushes his conga far away from him. Clearly, his coping style during the session has been one of evasiveness – but he deployed this style in such a way that he attracted a lot of attention.

Mr R takes on a different strategy. He starts by showing off his musical talent while playing the drum kit. Yet, his verbal reactions and his musical reactions do not match. For example, Mr R declares 'I played very well on the single first instrument that came across', while in fact he switched three times to a different instrument and he did not participate in the first assignments. He tries to bond with the dominant Mr C, and laughs at all the jokes of Mr C, thus adding fuel to the flames in the group. Clearly, Mr R's coping style is to show off and to bond with a person who seems to be 'stronger', and reducing his tension by making cynical remarks and laughter.

Mr S plays the drums very carefully. He is very attentive to what the others do, and adjusts to all their changes. However, he appears to forget to listen to himself. Although his playing, laughing and speaking is very soft and gentle, he is capable of saying what he would like to change so the group can play better together. Clearly, his coping style is to adjust to any other person, thus losing touch with himself. Although he does not ask for attention, when he gets the attention he is able to speak up.

Stage 3 – recognition

The goal of the third stage in the music therapy programme is to help clients recognise their personal coping strategies, using elaborate musical coursework. The music therapist assists the client in formulating treatment goals and objectives for change. Together with the client, the music therapist links the client's personal coping strategies to his experiences in daily life, and makes the transfer to the high-risk situations under which substance abuse occurs.

Clients are subjected to many different musical situations, to recognise their unique personal pitfalls and strengths in all these different circumstances. For this stage, one of the most commonly used musical styles is popular music. The music therapist works with music listening (e.g. Horesh 2006a) as well as with playing improvised music, composed (popular) music as well as rap music therapy (e.g. Hakvoort 2008).

Musical interventions can be described in terms of the structuring, empathetic, confronting, redirecting and emotion-exploring musical techniques as described by Bruscia (1987). If repetitive patterns of a client's behaviour appear in different musical situations, the therapist could attribute this repetitive pattern to the personal coping strategy of the client.

One of the tools to support and improve an unbiased verbal feedback and discussion about these musical behaviours to clients is video-registration of the sessions. Such registrations help clients to review and rehear their musical performances and coping mechanisms applied. In a later stage, the video helps the client to improve his insight and self-reflection on his behaviour. Video-registration also motivates clients to explicitly monitor their progress during the music therapy treatment programme.

EXAMPLE OF STAGE 3 – RECOGNITION

Mr G is a 40-year-old man with a serious drinking problem: he alternates sober periods with extreme alcohol abuse. During his drinking episodes he behaves very aggressively, and has caused a lot of problems in his social environment (work, family, friends and neighbourhood). When he is drunk, he expresses that he is 'angry with the world'.

During the music therapy he is always friendly and cooperative. He always follows the initiatives of other clients. He restricts himself to whatever someone else wants, even if he has ideas and preferences of his own. With such a strategy, Mr G has no social problems at all. While playing music in assignments 5 and 7 of the second stage, he follows up all assignments and conforms to all the dynamic patterns of other group members. He starts to develop his own initiatives but, as soon as someone else prompts another idea, Mr G conforms again. During verbal discussions, he does not recognise, or is even aware of, this subordinate behaviour. During the exercises, his interactions appear to be limited to adjustment, while his coping strategies are limited to denial and evasiveness.

While Mr G plays his solo, two other clients play terribly loud and are not even aware of Mr G's efforts. The other group members are very irritated by the loud playing of the other two. After the improvisation, Mr G declares: 'I did not hear the loud playing; it did not affect my playing, and if it did, it did not bother me.' Mr G appears to be unable to register what is going on, and (at least partly) deploys a coping strategy of denial.

During stage 3, the group watch the video-registration of this improvisation. It clearly shows the (re)actions of Mr G. He starts to play; when his invitation to play is not confirmed by the two others, his body freezes and the intensity of his musical performance fades away. The more he freezes his movement and play, the more tension is visible in his mimics. The group interprets this facial expression as being angry. Mr G, who watched the video too, makes a direct transfer to his personal coping style. Due to the fact that he denies, ignores and trivialises his social environment, he builds up a lot of stress and tension and consequently feels frustrated about everything. He recognises his tensions, and labels them as being his high-risk situations for maintaining his drinking habit. Clearly, drinking is his coping strategy to reduce any anxiety evoked by his denial. Only while drunk is he able to really feel, and express, his anger.

Stage 4 – experimenting with new coping strategies

After the client has decided on which treatment goals to pursue, he has to practise and learn new coping skills to deal with his personal high-risk situations. The music therapist guides him in choosing his own musical tools to achieve changes. The objective of the fourth stage in the music therapy programme is to teach the client to adopt new coping skills and to assist him in handling those skills in specific circumstances. The goals of this stage vary to a large degree between different clients due to differences in their own coping skills. For example, a client who used psychoactive substances as a coping strategy to reduce discomfort might want to learn to use music as a tool to express his emotions better. Other clients, who used substances to encourage themselves towards situation-oriented behaviour, might want to learn to use music to act in stressful situations without the necessity of using drugs. Mr G, for example, chose to use music to learn to express himself and to be aware of his own feelings. He used his voice in different assignments to achieve this goal.

Stage 5 – termination and evaluation

The goal of this last stage in the music therapy programme is to help the client to acknowledge his new coping strategies and to recognise how and when to use them in a transfer to his daily life. Of course, this stage is meant as the round-off stage in the programme, with all the usual conventions.

Discussion

Music therapy offers concrete help for clients who suffer from addiction problems by offering the potential to (re)gain better coping strategies. Music offers a client the possibility to act in a structured, joyful and safe environment. A well-trained music therapist is capable of manipulating musical situations which offer the proper confronting experiences that provide clients insight in – and practical exercise with – their coping styles and strategies. A client has to show behavioural patterns that prove he can deal with different situations in different ways, and thus has alternative patterns of behaviour in high-risk situations than to use narcotics or alcohol.

Music therapy treatment places clients in situations that show strong similarities with their daily life. Yet, the musical context makes the experience of these situations distinctively different. This enables a client to recognise and reconsider his conditions, and the choices he makes in real life, in a more distanced and safe context. The musical context helps him to gain insight into his coping strategies, because it involves no direct personal consequences if he falls short. By nature, music turns out to be a strong motivating force.

The music therapist must stimulate the client to make explicit transfers from his experiences in the musical situations and processes to situations in his daily life. In particular, the music therapy promotes the application of new coping strategies in high-risk situations that otherwise trigger substance abuse.

The music therapy programme offers the therapist a well-focused, goal-oriented and musical method to help clients assess, and maybe overcome, some of their major problems with substance abuse. It affects the overt behaviour and coping skills of substance abusers, and offers clients better insights and understanding of their own actual behaviour and reactions.

As stated at the beginning of the chapter, substance abuse is a very complex and chronic problem. Most of the clients will experience (major) relapses, especially if the treatment focuses only on the particular topic of enhancing coping strategies. We must realise that coping styles are only a small part of the complex mechanisms that must be addressed during multidisciplinary treatment of addiction problems.

While building experience with this methodology, the authors increasingly find indications that music therapy affects the same neurological paths as some substances do. Music triggers a sense of well-being and strong emotions, and it can stimulate craving as well as motivation. Further research is absolutely necessary to find more evidence for the connections between musical stimuli and the neurological paths that lead to substance abuse, and for the proper interventions that could restore the flawed reward system of substance abusers.

CHAPTER 6

Music Therapy with Chemically Dependent Clients: A Relapse Prevention Model

Ted Ficken

Introduction

This chapter presents a discussion of how music therapists can use music interventions to reinforce relapse prevention concepts. Drawing from my 35 years of experience as a music therapist, I will describe characteristics of relapsers and non-relapsers, and how music can be used along the treatment continuum to assist clients who are trying to recover from the harmful aspects of addiction. My experience includes working directly with inpatients in hospitals and residential treatment facilities in the United States—in the states of California, Kansas, Oregon, Minnesota, and Arizona. Some of that work included coordination of aftercare programs for clients fresh out of residential treatment. I have also supervised other music therapists and music therapy interns working with this population and have presented on this topic at national and regional music therapy conferences in both the United States and Canada. I have designed and led workshops on uses of music and art therapies to groups of chemical dependency counselors, art therapists, and music therapists.

Addictions are often described along a continuum from use, to misuse, to abuse, to dependency. This may apply to addictions to alcohol, drugs, tobacco, sex, food, or any number of potentially harmful substances or behaviors. In this chapter I will focus primarily on chemicals—drugs, alcohol, and tobacco. People who seek help along this continuum, or are forced to seek help, are faced with the reality of trying to reduce harm to both themselves and to those people around them. I say, "forced to seek help," because involuntary treatment has been found to be effective in many cases. I say, "reduce harm," because problems with addiction, without exception, harm relationships, physical health, mental health, spiritual well-being, vocational and financial stability, and general quality of life.

The treatment continuum for this population ranges from self-help books, to self-help groups, to outpatient settings, to inpatient or residential settings, to aftercare settings. Depending on the type of setting, consumers of services are commonly referred to as substance abusers, the chemically dependent or, increasingly, as persons with co-occurring disorders, or having dual diagnoses. The latter two labels are used to describe individuals who may have a mental illness, exacerbated by problems with addictions or, in some cases, additional problems with developmental disabilities. In this chapter, for simplicity, I will use the terms "client(s)" and "chemical dependency" to refer to individuals with these types of problems. It is not my intent to label these individuals in a negative way. In treatment settings, labels are often necessary for the purpose of billing insurance companies or payment and reimbursement sources.

Readers are encouraged to think of their clients as human beings, who are experiencing difficulties, each with his or her own story. Resist the temptation to label, stereotype, or otherwise stigmatize the people you work with. While this chapter will not focus on music therapy assessment strategies, effective treatment can only be initiated following a thorough assessment, as specified by music therapy professional standards of practice. By completing comprehensive assessments, music therapists will learn their clients' individual stories.

A common theme along both the addiction and treatment continuums is relapse prevention. Individuals are provided with knowledge, skills, and abilities to help them refrain from self-destructive behaviors, recover from any damage done, and get on with their lives. In some cases, total abstinence from the harmful behaviors is stressed, while in other cases the focus may be on learning to moderate the behavior to reduce harm to self or others. If chemical dependency is sometimes a downward spiral, spinning out of control until a person hits "rock bottom," then relapse prevention is a set of tools to interrupt that spiral, or prevent it from starting in the first place.

Music therapists are trained to use music as a tool to help others. Music therapy goals are usually related to maintenance or improvement of functioning within a domain. For example, domains may include cognitive or mental functioning, physical functioning, social functioning, or spiritual functioning. All of these domains are relevant to settings dealing with chemical dependency clients, and to relapse prevention. In various settings, the application of music might be referred to as music activities, practices, interventions, experiences, treatments, reinforcers, or by some other program-specific term. For the purpose of this chapter, I will use the term "intervention." For me, intervention has come to mean a music therapy approach, as specified in a written treatment care plan, to assist a client in reaching short-term and long-term personal recovery goals.

As music therapists complete academic and clinical training programs, and enter the world of music therapy employment or practice, they are often faced with adapting the theories and interventions that they have learned to pre-existing and, in some cases, well-established treatment programs. The question becomes, "How can I use my music therapy skills to align with the mission, vision, and values of this program?" Music therapy cannot be practiced in a vacuum, an island unto itself. It should be carefully integrated into any program, to coordinate with, support, and reinforce overall treatment program objectives. For example, a music therapist working in a common 30-day residential chemical dependency treatment program, built around the 12 steps of Alcoholic Anonymous, should select short-term interventions that reinforce the 12 steps. Another music therapist, working in a long-term (six months or more) program that is focused on harm reduction, will have the luxury of additional time to work with his or her clients, and can select interventions that may require more time to successfully reach goals related to harm reduction. As we will see later in this chapter, adopting a music therapy relapse prevention structure affords flexibility to tailor music therapy interventions to fit any length or type of program.

In the following sections of this chapter, I will first look at relapse prevention concepts. What are the behaviors commonly found in individuals who do not relapse? Next, I take a brief and simple inventory of typical music therapy interventions. What types of music therapy approaches can be found in many clinical settings? Finally, I will present examples of integration, to illustrate how music therapy interventions can be adapted to facilitate desired behaviors and concepts that reinforce and support relapse prevention.

Relapse prevention

Certain behaviors, characteristics, and attributes seem to be present in clients who do not relapse into past, destructive behaviors. I will discuss 16 of these qualities (summarized in Table 6.1). Addiction is often described as a baffling disease, and the presence of these characteristics, attributes, or behaviors does not guarantee that a client will not relapse. Studies show that alcoholics and drug addicts have a high relapse rate, and that some clients complete multiple courses of treatment before they establish a recovery program that works for them. However, I have observed that using music therapy interventions to teach, practice, support, and reinforce relapse prevention behaviors can produce positive treatment outcomes. Let's look at 16 relapse prevention concepts.

Non-relapsers have a toolkit of effective coping skills. These might include skills in anger management, stress reduction/relaxation, effective communication and negotiation, assertiveness, healthy feeling expression, or decision-making. Not only do non-relapsers have these skills, but also they regularly use them. They might count to ten when angry, take deep breaths when they are feeling anxious, set aside time to talk to family members or friends, stand up for themselves when appropriate, or have creative outlets for their feelings. They do not hold things in, or isolate from others. They cope well when life throws them curves or barriers.

A second attribute is that non-relapsers have a high degree of self-efficacy. They believe in themselves, and their ability to make positive choices and changes. If they have a lapse, they usually attribute the lapse to the situation, not to themselves. A lapse, in this case, would be a single slip into a past, undesirable behavior. When lapses are repeated, they turn into relapses. Non-relapsers do not think of themselves as weak, lacking conviction, or unable to change. They believe in themselves.

My observation is that non-relapsers attend and involve themselves in a 12-step program, such as Alcoholics or Narcotics Anonymous, or any other structure such as Friends of Sobriety (http://friendsofsobriety.com?Home_Page.html) (Humphreys et al. 2004; Marlatt and Gordon 1985, p.458). They do more than just attend meetings. They seek out a sponsor, ask for help, and use the support of their group. They use the 12 steps, or similar structure, as the framework for how they live their lives. They work the program.

Alcoholics and drug addicts seem to exhibit depressive characteristics, and alcohol is a depressant. Non-relapsers have learned how to recognize and deal with depression. They develop an attitude of optimism and hope. A "can do" mind-set replaces a "can't/won't do" line of thought. There is a commitment to positive change.

My experience indicates that most successful non-relapsers set a goal of abstinence from their addictive substance or behavior. I understand that others feel that a harm reduction approach is more realistic, but I have never been a fan of teaching alcoholics or drug addicts to use alcohol or drugs in moderation, or in some controlled way. If something can potentially lead to your death, and it causes profound pain in the lives of others, I believe it should be avoided entirely. I recommend abstinence. This becomes tricky with addictions to food or sex, but clients can still learn to abstain from certain foods, or quantities of foods, and avoid specific, risky sexual behaviors. I admit it is a gray area, but I have seen clients successfully achieve recovery by abstaining.

As mentioned above, lapses are common, but tend to be non-repeating events. Non-relapsers recognize this, and are able to learn from a lapse and move on. With them, it is not "all or nothing." A one-time slip does not automatically deteriorate into a full-blown relapse.

There have been several popular songs with the title, "One Day at a Time," and this sentiment illustrates the next non-relapser quality: maintaining a proximal focus. Non-relapsers are not overwhelmed by thinking that they must give up a previous behavior for their entire life. They are more focused on making it through the next hour, or the next day. Making good decisions and choices in the present replaces thinking about large spans of time, sometimes called distal thinking. Proximal trumps distal.

Non-relapsers work at improving relationships, and have strong marital and family cohesion. This is why many treatment programs include a family education, or family therapy, component. The goal is to understand family dynamics, enabling behaviors, co-dependency, and other relationship issues. Non-relapsers try to make amends to family members and repair broken relationships. They work at rebuilding trust and mutual support.

In addition to 12-step groups and family support, non-relapsers build extended networks. As the number of committed supporters grows, the chance of maintaining a clean and sober lifestyle also increases. The support network might include co-workers, supervisors, neighbors, church members, fellow club members, or others. Non-relapsers stop isolating, and begin to network and cultivate connections with a variety of other people. Gaining comfort in groups can be an important treatment goal.

Certain things in the environment can become strong triggers for substance use, misuse, abuse, and dependency. Smells, sounds, people, locations, and music can all be cues to engage in harmful, risky behaviors. While conducting a workshop with chemical dependency counselors, I played the Pink Floyd song, "Comfortably Numb." My intent was to use the song as an example of songs that illustrate harmful effects of drug use. One of the workshop participants, a certified drug and alcohol counselor, who was also a recovering addict, began to have flashbacks to memories of her drug use days and broke into a cold sweat. She found herself immediately craving her drug of choice. She was able to excuse herself from the workshop and made her way to a nearby 12-step meeting, but the experience taught me how powerful music can be as a reminder or trigger of drug-related behaviors—both psychologically and physically. Non-relapsers either avoid known cues, including some music, or learn to reframe those environmental factors. Reframing involves pairing new information with those triggers, and forming new associations.

While working at a treatment facility in Arizona, I offered lectures on the uses of music in recovery. One client, upon leaving treatment and returning to New York City, reported a post-treatment experience to me. He returned to his place of employment and, after one week, received a paycheck. He said that having money in his pocket triggered a desire to go to downtown Manhattan in search of a drug dealer. However, as he was walking down the street, he passed a bar where he could hear the jukebox through an open door. The record on the turntable was Neil Young's "The Needle and the Damage Done," which I had used in my music and recovery lecture. He said that hearing the song reminded him of what he had learned in treatment, and instead of seeking out a dealer, he sought out a 12-step meeting. At least for that night, he made it home without using drugs, and music had played a role in his decision-making process. Non-relapsers avoid or reframe cues and triggers.

Recovery does not miraculously appear after a stay in a treatment facility, be it a 30-day program or longer. Participation in an aftercare program is a prominent feature of non-relapsers. In Arizona, I made sure that all clients had an aftercare program lined up as they left our treatment facility, no matter where in the US they were returning.

As clients take their first steps into recovery, and put treatment experiences into practice, new behaviors must be reinforced. Non-relapsers reward themselves for good behavior and choices. Rewards do not need to be large or expensive, nor do they need to be materialistic. I have had clients who have rewarded themselves with time with their spouse or children, going to a movie, purchasing new clothes, taking a trip, taking a nap, getting a massage, playing their guitar, or buying a new piece of recording equipment.

Taking good care of one's physical self is the next non-relapser characteristic. This includes participating in physical exercise, eating a healthy diet, getting enough sleep, and seeking medical attention when needed. Alcoholism and drug addiction can take their toll on a person's physical condition. Recovery needs to include regaining physical health and establishing a regimen of ongoing self-care habits.

The next quality of non-relapsers is having a healthy spiritual life. This means different things to different people. For some, it is practicing a faith or religion, returning to a former place of worship, and participating in a community based around certain beliefs. For others, it is developing a spiritual life, centered in an understanding that there are powers greater than one's self (Marlatt and Donovan 2005, p.171). Spirituality is often described as finding a purpose in life, serving others, developing a sense of morality, or just plain trying to be a better person.

Non-relapsers are employed more than relapsers. They have a job. The structure of having a working environment, including having a stable income to live on, seems to help clients resist slipping into past, negative behaviors. Especially in early recovery, structure of any kind in a person's day-to-day life appears to strengthen resolve, and adds to a feeling of accomplishment and self-worth.

Finally, when non-relapsers are engaged in discussions about their recovery, they tend to focus more on positive behavior changes, and less on retelling stories related to previous drinking or drugging episodes. There is no bragging about outrageous behaviors committed under the influence. Instead, there is a focus on positive change and growth.

The 16 characteristics described above are found more in non-relapsers than in relapsers, and although these factors are no guarantee of success, they should be encouraged during treatment. Table 6.1 summarizes these characteristics, and shows the differences between people who relapse and those who do not.

Table 6.1 Relapse prevention behaviors

Non-relapsers	Relapsers
1. Have developed a repertoire of coping skills: decision-making, cognitive restructuring, refuting, stress reduction, communication, assertiveness, feeling expression	1. Either don't have or don't use coping skills
2. Have a high degree of self-efficacy; believe in self; attribute lapses to the situation	2. Don't believe in self; attribute lapses to self-failure
3. Attend and involve themselves in a recovery program; get a sponsor; ask for help; work the program	3. Don't work a program; try to do it alone
4. Positive attitude; handle depression; have a "can do" attitude; commit to change	4. Negative attitude; tendency to be depressed; pessimistic; "can't do," or "won't do," mind-set; lack commitment
5. Goal is abstinence	5. Goal is controlled use
6. Bounce back from lapses; a lapse is a one-time event	6. Turn lapses into relapses
7. Proximal focus; "one day at a time"	7. Distal focus; are overwhelmed by maintenance for long periods of time
8. Marital and family cohesion; healthy relationships	8. Marital, family, and relationship discord
9. Have a developed support system, beyond recovery program	9. Limited network
10. Avoid or reframe old cues; establish new cues and associations	10. Respond to old cues
11. Attend aftercare	11. Drop out of aftercare
12. Reward themselves for successful change	12. Punish themselves for failure; don't give themselves credit for success
13. Participate in a program of physical self-care (exercise, sleep, nutrition)	13. Sedentary; don't exercise; poor eating habits; poor sleeping habits
14. Have a spiritual life; attend church	14. No sense of spirituality; do not attend church
15. Employed	15. Unemployed
16. Talk focused on behavior changes	16. Talk focused on drug/alcohol "war" stories; retelling stories about drinking/drugging

Music therapy interventions

Before I give examples of music interventions that can reinforce relapse prevention concepts, let's begin with a brief review of common music therapy practices. In general, music can be performed, listened to, conceptualized, composed, written or read about, and verbalized about.

The music, in and of itself, can have a therapeutic effect. As music therapists, we know that the relationship between therapist and client(s) is also an important element. Music interventions must be carefully selected by a trained therapist, expertly introduced and facilitated and, whenever possible, generalized to non-musical content through careful processing.

Performance interventions include such things as improvisation using tunable instruments, drum circles or other percussion activities, instrumental or vocal performance ensembles, solo music performing, moving or dancing to music, or toning. For some clients, music performance may be a vocation or prominent avocation, and stabilizing those functional areas is desired.

Listening strategies include listening to music for relaxation or stress reduction, guided imagery with music to uncover and process extra-musical information, vibrotactile stimulation, or even physically exercising to music. Clients are not actually performing music, but they are listening to it, attending to its effects, and applying it.

Conceptual strategies include musical games, instrumental or vocal lessons, uses of music in leisure time, or discussing music theories. The idea is to learn about music concepts, and in therapy the emphasis is on generalizing the learning behavior to non-musical goals.

Musical composition can be a potent tool in therapy. Clients can compose original music, write songs, work out arrangements, orchestrate melodies, and make recording decisions. I have found songwriting to be especially potent with my clients. The process of writing a song provides opportunities to think about various topics; represent those thoughts lyrically; create and modify melodies, rhythms, and textures; and produce a lasting product. Once created, a song can be used again and again to remind, reinforce, and relive.

Music can be written or read about. Examples may be reading books about prominent musicians (especially musicians who are in a successful recovery program), reading articles about music analysis or critiques, reading reviews of concerts, watching public service announcements by musicians, or merely keeping a musical journal. Some clients may even write their own musical autobiography, or create a life review, complete with musical soundtrack.

Lyric discussions are a good example of verbalizing about music. With the availability of large quantities of digital music, music therapists do not need to search very far to find songs on almost any topic. By carefully selecting songs with relevant lyrics, music therapists can stimulate new thought, introduce subjects, facilitate catharsis, and use music to create new associations and reminders. For clients who may be threatened by music performance, there may be some comfort in listening to music and discussing lyrics. Clients will find songs that they can identify with, or explain how their lives are different from the artist's expression.

Many music therapy interventions are a combination of these approaches. Clients may perform, listen to, conceptualize about, compose, and verbalize about music all during the course of a single treatment group. But how can these common music therapy approaches be used in a chemical dependency relapse prevention model? How can music therapists adapt their knowledge, skills, and abilities to fit pre-existing program content? How can music therapy approaches and relapse prevention approaches be integrated?

Different treatment settings and client populations call for different music therapy approaches. Some settings may use a predominant approach. For example, one setting may use a Nordoff and Robbins approach (Nordoff and Robbins 2007), another setting may use a Orff Schulwerk approach, (Bitcon 2000) a third setting may stress Michael Thaut's neurological music therapy model (Thaut, Nickel and Hömberg 2004), and still another setting might emphasize Helen Bonny's method of guided imagery with music (Bonny 2002). I have found that chemical dependency settings call for a flexible, eclectic approach. While clients may be impaired by their chemical use, once in a controlled, chemical-free setting, they frequently reconstitute rapidly. They may be perceived as high functioning, and are capable of active participation with music in a variety of ways. They are also frequently capable of extensive verbal processing of their musical experiences.

Table 6.2 provides a model for integration. By listing the music therapy approaches along the vertical axis, and relapse prevention behaviors along the horizontal axis, we establish a framework for creating, adapting, categorizing, and planning music therapy interventions in chemical dependency treatment settings. If we assign numbers to the music therapy strategies, and letters to the relapse prevention strategies, we see a model emerge to integrate the two approaches. Music interventions can be thought of as A1 strategies, C10 strategies, F15 strategies, and so on, each intervention using a music approach to teach, practice, or reinforce a relapse prevention behavior or concept. In the next section, I will present examples and case studies to illustrate how this integration is put into practice. I will present enough examples to illustrate this integrated approach, but each individual music therapist can add his or her own repertoire of interventions to the model.

Not all cells in Table 6.2 will be appropriate for developing interventions. For example, musical games might not be a good fit to reinforce spirituality. Therapists are encouraged to use the table as an organizational and planning tool. Therapists should be flexible in using pre-planned interventions. As therapy sessions progress, therapists must be willing to adapt, deviate from, and adjust interventions in response to client needs and responses. Caution must be used to select interventions that match client readiness and stages of change.

The framework of Table 6.2 allows for flexibility when planning a series of treatment groups or interventions. A music therapist might have a songwriting group, using song creation to reinforce all of the relapse prevention concepts, or a therapist might have an emotional regulation group, addressing issues related to depression, and utilizing a variety of music interventions beyond songwriting. The model presented in the table then becomes a model to categorize interventions, and serves as a method for planning groups and individual sessions.

Examples of music therapy interventions related to relapse prevention

As I present examples, I will identify them by the corresponding letter and number from Table 6.2. For example, an A1 example would be a songwriting activity to work on the development of coping skills. A C3 example would illustrate a drumming activity to learn about a structured recovery program, such as Alcoholics Anonymous. An H9 intervention might utilize a singing activity to learn about family relationships. You get the idea.

Example 1: A drumming activity to learn about a structured recovery program (C3)

Patrick Pinson, owner of Cedar Mountain Drums in Portland, Oregon, has provided drumming workshops and drum circles in a variety of clinical settings. In an article he published in 1991, he described a drum circle he had conducted on a chemical dependency treatment unit for adult males who had volunteered for treatment as a way to gain early release from the prison system. Patrick began the drum circle by providing a steady beat, and then asked each individual to express his own rhythm. After 45

Table 6.2 Integration of music interventions and relapse prevention concepts

		A. Develop coping skills	B. High degree of self-efficacy	C. Attend and participate in recovery program	D. Positive attitude, low depression, optimistic, "can do," commitment to change	E. Abstinence	F. Bounce back from lapses	G. Proximal focus: one day at a time	H. Marital, family, relationship cohesion	I. Strong support network	J. Avoid or reframe old cues	K. Attend aftercare	L. Reward self for success	M. Active physical self-care	N. Spiritual life/church	O. Employed	P. Focus on behavior change talk
1.	Songwriting	A1	B1	C1	D1	E1	F1	G1	H1	I1	J1	K1	L1	M1	N1	O1	P1
2.	Improvisation	A2	B2	C2	D2	E2	F2	G2	H2	I2	J2	K2	L2	M2	N2	O2	P2
3.	Drumming	A3	B3	C3	D3	E3	F3	G3	H3	I3	J3	K3	L3	M3	N3	O3	P3
4.	Group performance	A4	B4	C4	D4	E4	F4	G4	H4	I4	J4	K4	L4	M4	N4	O4	P4
5.	Musical games	A5	B5	C5	D5	E5	F5	G5	H5	I5	J5	K5	L5	M5	N5	O5	P5
6.	Exercise to music	A6	B6	C6	D6	E6	F6	G6	H6	I6	J6	K6	L6	M6	N6	O6	P6
7.	Movement or dance	A7	B7	C7	D7	E7	F7	G7	H7	I7	J7	K7	L7	M7	N7	O7	P7

	A. Develop coping skills	B. High degree of self-efficacy	C. Attend and participate in recovery program	D. Positive attitude, low depression, optimistic, "can do," commitment to change	E. Abstinence	F. Bounce back from lapses	G. Proximal focus: one day at a time	H. Marital, family, relationship cohesion	I. Strong support network	J. Avoid or reframe old cues	K. Attend aftercare	L. Reward self for success	M. Active physical self-care	N. Spiritual life/church	O. Employed	P. Focus on behavior change talk
8. Lyric discussions	A8	B8	C8	D8	E8	F8	G8	H8	I8	J8	K8	L8	M8	N8	O8	P8
9. Instrument or voice	A9	B9	C9	D9	E9	F9	G9	H9	I9	J9	K9	L9	M9	N9	O9	P9
10. Relaxation/de-stress	A10	B10	C10	D10	E10	F10	G10	H10	I10	J10	K10	L10	M10	N10	O10	P10
11. Guided imagery	A11	B11	C11	D11	E11	F11	G11	H11	I11	J11	K11	L11	M11	N11	O11	P11
12. Toning	A12	B12	C12	D12	E12	F12	G12	H12	I12	J12	K12	L12	M12	N12	O12	P12
13. Leisure music	A13	B13	C13	D13	E13	F13	G13	H13	I13	J13	K13	L13	M13	N13	O13	P13
14. Music as a vocation	A14	B14	C14	D14	E14	F14	G14	H14	I14	J14	K14	L14	M14	N14	O14	P14
15. Vibrotactile stimulation	A15	B15	C15	D15	E15	F15	G15	H15	I15	J15	K15	L15	M15	N15	O15	P15

minutes of uninterrupted drumming, Patrick facilitated a verbal processing session. He described that session:

> Each member of the circle shared from the heart. The common theme of the sharing was a sense of peacefulness. Some commented that their anger was lifted or pushed down. Others reported a sense of serenity that they had never felt before. I felt honored to sit in that circle. My tension had eased and I felt at one with the group. I offered a closing prayer to adjourn the circle. The residents lined up and nurtured Steve and I with hugs and expressions of gratitude. Steve suggested that they keep the silence for the rest of the evening. Together, the drumming circle had indeed created a sacred space. (Pinson 1991, p.9)

After reading several of Patrick's articles, I invited him to participate in one of my workshops, where he led a drum circle with chemical dependency counselors, music therapists, and art therapists. As I watched him work, and participated in his process, it gave me the idea to use a drum circle in a different way with my clients, to reinforce recovery program concepts.

Based on my work experience, I knew that many recovery programs utilize slogans, or catch phrases, as reminders for key concepts. I began by making a list of some of these phrases, such as "pity pot," "one day at a time," "I can't, he can, I think I'll let him," "let go, let god," "fake it, 'til you make it," "stinkin' thinkin'," "keep coming back," and "it works if you work it." These were common recovery phrases that I had heard frequently in the programs where I worked.

With a group of male clients, new to treatment, I facilitated a drum circle, but then told them that I wanted to try something different. I divided the group into pairs, giving each pair one of the slogans, written on a piece of paper. I then asked them to create a rhythm to fit their slogan. After allowing time for them to experiment and come up with a rhythm, I instructed each pair to add their rhythm, one at a time, around the circle. As each new rhythm was added, the overall group composition became more complex, with some phrases introducing different accents and syncopations. Group members appeared to enjoy the intervention, and there was a feeling of fun and community. As I brought the drumming to a close, I asked each group member to talk about their experience, including their thoughts on the assigned phrase. What did the phrase mean to him? Why was it relevant to his treatment? I had begun, through the music activity, to facilitate comfort in a group, introduce some program concepts, and engage new clients into a group process. For some of the group members it was their first experience talking about treatment, what it meant to them, their feelings, and their hopes.

Although I did not record the session, that is an option. The "catch phrase drum circle" could be recorded and used later as the basis for a songwriting activity, relaxation session, musical game, or guided imagery. I have found that using my clients' own creations in later groups and sessions can be very potent. When combined with non-musical information, such as the catch phrases, the music can strengthen associations and reminders.

Example 2: A lyric analysis activity to introduce concepts of harm reduction and the effects of chemical dependency on relationships (H8)

In April 1999 a group of researchers, sponsored by the Office of National Drug Control Policy and the Department of Health and Human Services' Substance Abuse and Mental Health Services Administration, published an article about substance abuse references in popular movies and songs (Roberts, Henriksen and Christenson 1999). The study examined 1000 of the most popular songs from 1996 to 1997. Twenty-seven percent of the songs contained references to either alcohol or illicit drugs, but only 19 percent of the songs mentioned negative consequences. Only 42 songs mentioned consequences of either drug or alcohol use. A similar study, published in 2008 by a group of researchers at the University of Pittsburgh School of Medicine, analyzed the top 279 songs on the Billboard charts in 2005 (Primack *et al.* 2008). Thirty-three percent of those songs made reference to drugs and alcohol, but only four songs contained anti-use messages. Reading these research articles challenged me to try to find a way to use music to illustrate the harmful effects of music, both on individuals and on relationships.

I began by going through my own collection of recordings to find songs that might illustrate the harmful effects of either drugs or alcohol. I was working with adult clients, so I focused on age-appropriate songs, considering music preferences of my group members. After a prolonged search, I came up with a list of songs that included the following: "I Want a New Drug" by Huey Lewis and the News, portraying physical illness and car accidents; "Wasted on the Way" by Crosby, Stills, Nash and Young, illustrating loss of time, "Alcohol" by the Kinks, presenting family problems, loss of income, loss of home; "Please, Daddy" by John Denver, which paints a picture of family pain; and "The No No Song" by Ringo Starr, a humorous portrayal of loss of coordination and physical illness while under the influence of alcohol or drugs. There were other songs. Present readers will need to search for more current songs, in genres that appeal to their clients.

Once I assembled the songs, I explained to my treatment group that I had planned a music listening activity for the day. I gave a brief discussion, citing some of the research about popular songs. I challenged them to see if they could find content in the songs that illustrated possible harmful effects of either drug or alcohol use. I gave them lyric sheets and highlighter pens, and asked them to highlight any section of each song that they felt illustrated a consequence of drug or alcohol use. We listened to each song, stopping to discuss their findings after each song. At first, the group members seemed reluctant to participate, almost appearing to want to deny that there could be any possible negative consequences of drug or alcohol behaviors. However, as the activity moved from song to song, a sense of competition and confrontation emerged. Group members competed to be the first to find the negative consequences in each song, and also began to make comments to each other about their own negative consequences. Some were surprised that some of their favorite songs actually contained anti-drug messages.

In other, non-music therapy groups, certified addiction counselors were also presenting information about the negative consequences of addictive behaviors. They reported to me that group members referred to some of the songs from my group, and were able to relate the lecture information to the songs. The songs took on new meaning, with associations related to the harmful effects of drugs and alcohol on individuals and relationships.

Example 3: Exercising to music to practice physical self-care (M6)

A fellow music therapist, who I greatly admire, once said to me, "I don't do exercise groups. I'm a music therapist." The point was that we had other staff, recreational therapists, who conducted exercise and fitness classes. It was a professional turf issue. I disagreed. My disagreement was based on two thoughts. First, I considered exercising to music a valid music therapy approach. Music was being used as a tool to promote maintenance or improvement in the physical domain. Music provided structure, increased motivation, could be selected to challenge and increase stamina, added enjoyment, and facilitated movement. Participants experienced increased heart rates, increased oxygen intake, decreased galvanic skin response, and other benefits. My second thought was that it was a perfect chance to collaborate with another discipline—modeling cooperative behavior, good relationships, and asking for help from others—all related to relapse prevention concepts. Since the recreation therapist was offering exercise and fitness groups without music, I saw an opportunity to share skills, learn about each other's discipline, and create a group experience that combined approaches.

In my personal life, I attend classes at a local gym. These include weight training classes and spinning classes on stationary bicycles. All of the classes are structured around carefully selected music, nine songs to each hour-long class. I believe that providing similar music-based classes in treatment can help clients improve in the physical domain, and can also serve as a bridge to the community, where they can have access to both public and private gyms.

I talked to the recreational therapist, asking if I could observe some of the exercise and fitness groups. He agreed. I learned his group process, the treatment goals in his groups, and observed how patients participated. Based on my visits, I identified ways in which music could be used to introduce exercise concepts, provide a soundtrack for exercises, make the workouts more effective, and increase the chances that clients would continue to exercise after leaving treatment.

Working with the recreational therapist, we decided that the group would be more successful if we worked with the clients to select preferred music. Over a course of many sessions, the clients listened to and selected music to fit each part of their workouts. They even made custom tapes of the music for themselves, to take with them when they left treatment.

Example 4: Music listening to teach counterarguing skills (B8)

Slater *et al.* (1996) published an article describing how they used TV beer advertisements in an alcohol education program with adolescents, to stimulate critical thought and teach counterarguing skills. This gave me an idea for a music intervention with my adult forensic clients. I did a search on the Internet and discovered that a CD was available of music used in television and radio advertisements.[1] A section of that CD included many advertising jingles related to alcohol and tobacco advertising. I decided to use the CD to challenge my clients' thinking errors, sometimes called cognitive distortions.

In the treatment program in the state hospital where I was working, clients came primarily from county jails. All of my clients had been charged with crimes, but had been found incompetent to stand trial, because of their mental illness. Our job was to restore them to competency, so that they could return to court and face their charges. Length of stay was typically 90 days or longer. The majority of clients had dual diagnoses—both a diagnosed

---

1   TeeVee Toons: The Commercials (1989), TVT Records, TVT 1400–2.

mental illness, and complications related to chemical dependency. While our focus was on restoration to competency, and preparing them to function within the legal system, we also had the opportunity to address their mental health and chemical dependency issues. One strong program emphasis was to look at thinking disorders. Borrowing from cognitive behavioral therapy approaches, we asked clients to look at how their perceptions of life, or misperceptions, had resulted in problems in their lives. Could they consider alternative ways of looking at things, which might help them avoid future problems or pain?

Knowing that my clients had been learning about thinking errors and cognitive distortions in some of their psychoeducational groups, I decided to use music to reinforce what they had learned, and strengthen their abilities to counterargue or refute false claims. By doing this, the treatment goal was to learn new coping skills, but also to strengthen feelings of self-efficacy. Before the music therapy session, I prepared manuscripts of the alcohol and tobacco advertising jingles. In the group session, we listened to the jingles and then discussed if there were any cognitive distortions present in the advertising. Did alcohol really add to friendships as the advertisements claimed? Were certain cigarettes better for you than others?

The jingles—some old, some more recent—were recognizable to the group members. They had heard them before, and remembered them. When they paid attention to the actual words in the jingles, they could see that many of the advertising claims were misleading or outright false. As we listened to the CD, there were many humorous comments made about the audacity of the advertisements' claims, but there were also some very serious comments made about the realities of drug and alcohol use. There were also negative comments made about the advertising industry, and their use of cognitive distortions to sway consumers. The intervention proved to be very successful, and similar activities were requested.

Example 5: A songwriting activity to reinforce 12-step concepts (C1)

In a journal article I published early in my career (Ficken 1976), I described a songwriting activity I used with chemical dependency clients. I was new to the field, and I was working at a state hospital facility where there was a small chemical dependency treatment program within a larger adult mental health program. Program management determined treatment schedules, and I found that I was assigned to provide a music therapy group to the chemical dependency clients several times a week. Program management did not dictate what I did in those groups. They assumed that I knew how to use music to benefit those clients. To be honest, the clients did not understand why they were receiving music therapy services, or how it could benefit them.

I knew that the program was built around the 12 steps of Alcoholics Anonymous. I also knew that clients new to treatment were often in a state of denial. Family members, employers, pastors, or others had frequently forced them into rehabilitation, but they did not believe that they had a problem, or if they did, they felt that they could control the problem without receiving help from others. I decided to try to use songwriting as a way to cut through that initial denial. If successful, I thought this would reinforce the first steps of both Alcoholics Anonymous and Narcotics Anonymous, the admission of powerlessness over alcohol and drugs and that their lives had become unmanageable.

I scoured my record collection at the time, and found a song by the Kinks, "Alcohol." The song is a melodramatic song about the slow destruction of a character's life due to the "demon alcohol." As the group of six clients came for their assigned music therapy group, I handed them a copy of the lyrics as they entered the small therapy room. They immediately began glancing at my handout, and with no introduction I played the song. They followed the lyrics as the song played. At its conclusion I simply asked if they felt that the song presented an accurate picture of alcoholism. There was an immediate reaction from the group. One of them actually stated, "That's not how I became an alcoholic." We spent the remainder of the session discussing the song, and many of the group members shared parts of their own stories. We brainstormed words and phrases that might be more representative of real alcoholism. At the conclusion of the session, I suggested that maybe we could use future sessions to work together as a group to write a more realistic song about alcoholism.

At the next session we worked together to construct an original song. One of the group members played guitar, and helped the group refine the melody and simple chord structure. They left the session, intent to work on their song outside of their scheduled groups. I gave them several days to work on the song, and then went to the unit with a tape recorder. We sat in the day room, in front of the program staff, and proceeded to rehearse and then record their song. In the matter of less than two weeks we had written and recorded a song that indicated a breakthrough in their system of denial. The song was then used in some of their other groups to reinforce the first step of Alcoholics Anonymous.

Discussion

Working with chemically dependent clients calls for music therapists to provide traditional music therapy interventions, but also to adapt some of those approaches to reinforce existing program design. Since relapse prevention is a core element of many chemical dependency treatment programs, using music to reinforce relapse prevention behaviors and concepts is recommended. A planning model that cross-references music interventions with relapse prevention ideas allows therapists to design and store intervention ideas.

I have presented a limited number of examples. Music therapists are encouraged to expand the ideas presented here, and to use the model to organize and plan their music therapy services for this population.

CHAPTER 7

Music Therapy as a Part of Drug Rehabilitation: From Adhering to Treatment to Integrating the Levels of Experience

Marko Punkanen

Introduction

Addiction is an interesting and in some ways also slightly mystical phenomenon. What makes a person become addicted to something? And how can one release oneself from an addiction? These questions have intrigued me for many years. As a clinician, I see drug addiction as a problem in a person's emotional life. It is important how a person is able to face, tolerate, name, and handle his or her emotions. In my experience it is important to understand that addiction is both physical and psychological. Therefore, treatment and care should have an effect on both levels, as well as offer the client comprehensive experiences. Additionally in my clinical experience, drug addicts quite often have traumatic experiences in their history and they will get in touch with their traumatic memories during the therapy process. Therefore, as a music therapist, I have to know how to work with my clients so that I can help them to increase their capacity for self-regulation and achieve more integration within their levels of experience. In this chapter, I will discuss the relationship between trauma and drug addiction and make some suggestions about how to integrate music therapy practices into the current practices of drug rehabilitation. My suggestions are based on results of personal research (Punkanen 2006a), where I interviewed four experienced Finnish music therapists who have worked in drug rehabilitation for many years. I have also included some quotes from the interviews for this chapter.

Drugs and drug addiction

Different kinds of psychoactive substances have been a part of humanity since the beginning of time. For example, from early on people learned about the effect plants have on human consciousness. Plants were used for example to alleviate pain and to tranquilize one's mind. Plants with these magical properties were for example the betel nut, leaves of the Khat (Catha edulis) and coca plants, cannabis, fly agarics and different kinds of cacti (Rätsch 2005).

The use of psychoactive plants had a strong social and ritualistic meaning. These substances were used in religious rituals and shamans to get into contact with the gods. Other participants in the rituals used the substances to strengthen the feeling of togetherness. Of course, these rituals had meaning for the individuals as well, as they offered them a chance to expand their consciousness (Ahlström 1998, p.21).

What does drug addiction mean and how is it defined? According to Reed (1994), drug addiction is often defined by using false arguments, such as how often drugs are used, which drugs are used, how large the doses are and how long the use has been going on. Although these are important factors to consider, they do not define the concept of drug addiction. According to Reed, addiction is not solely a question of continuous use of drugs, but is defined above all by the compulsive use of drugs, combined with loss of control of drug usage, denial of the problem and the continuation of use regardless of the negative consequences (Reed 1994, pp.7–11).

Affect regulation

There are many explanations for the causes of drug addiction. According to attachment and psychodynamic theories, the main problem seems to be a person's undeveloped affect regulation system (Schore 1994). That means that a person is unable to tolerate strong emotions, positive or negative. In these situations drugs can be used as a modulator of intolerable emotional state.

Self-regulatory capacities develop through early attachment relationships. The primary caregiver helps the child to regulate his or her arousal and emotional states through interactive regulation. When this finely attuned interaction between caregiver and the child is re-enacted appropriately time after time, it will expand the child's internalized template of safe relatedness and strengthen little by little the child's capacity to autoregulate his or her emotions (see e.g. Schore 1994; Siegel 1999). From Schore's (2003) perspective, "affect regulation is not just the reduction of affective intensity, the dampening of negative emotion. It also involves an amplification, an intensification of positive emotion, a condition necessary for more complex self-organization" (p.78). If interactive regulation doesn't work for some reason between caregiver and the child, or if a caregiver is not available for the child, it will leave the child alone with intolerable emotions. As an ongoing situation this will lead the child to internalize insecure or in worst cases disorganized–disoriented attachment patterns (see e.g. Ainsworth *et al.* 1978; Main and Hesse 1990). In these cases we can also talk about developmental trauma, which can mean emotional neglect and a constant feeling of insecurity.

In my research, the feeling of insecurity and intolerable emotions came up as the main causes for starting to use drugs. Young drug users stated that their parents weren't available for them, because of their own alcohol or mental health problems. They felt that they were left alone physically and emotionally. Then they started to look for security from peer groups and if drug use was part of the culture of that peer group they also started to use drugs to be accepted by that group. Intolerable emotions had their origin in growing up in families where some emotions were forbidden. In these situations the only solution was to deny and reject certain emotions (Punkanen 2006a, pp.77–79). When you try to learn as an adult to feel and express, for example, anger it can be a painful task, as one interviewed music therapist described:

> If there hasn't been anyone in childhood to tell the child that anger is part of life and to teach how to express and handle it, it will need a lot of therapeutic work when you are an adult and you try to learn to manage with it. In practice it can be totally intolerable if you feel that you are alone with it and you see drugs as the only relief in that situation. (Music therapist 1)

Maintaining a defensive wall against unacceptable and forbidden emotions requires a lot of time and energy. Drugs can become a relief for this kind of situation. When using drugs the control loosens and a person feels freer for a while.

Music therapy in trauma-related addiction treatment

In my research (Punkanen 2006a) and clinical practice, I define music therapy as a method of psychotherapeutic treatment. It creates strong sensorimotor and emotional experiences. Non-verbal music and/or sound vibration is combined with the verbal work that the client and therapist do together by reflecting on the experiences created by music and sound. The relation between music experiences and verbal experiences can vary both during a therapy session and for the whole duration of a treatment process (see e.g. Bruscia 1998).

In my research, it became obvious that addictive behavior is quite often an attempt to self-medicate trauma symptoms (Punkanen 2006a). There is already some evidence that trauma history increases risk for drug and alcohol use (see e.g. Kilpatrick *et al.* 1997; Miranda *et al.* 2002; Wilsnack *et al.* 1997). Compared to individuals without substance-use disorders, those with substance-use disorders report more traumatic events in their history (Cottler, Compton and Mager 1992). Among those seeking treatment for substance use disorders, 42–95 percent report histories of trauma (Berry and Sellman 2001; Brown, Read and Kahler 2003; Dansky, Byrne and Brady 1999). When drug addiction is a secondary disorder caused by unresolved trauma, the aim of the therapy should be an integration of dissociated and fragmented parts of the experience (emotions, sensations or thoughts). In this integrative work music therapy can be a motivating and rewarding modality. The possibilities and impacts that music therapy offers in the treatment of different kinds of addiction have been studied both in Finland and elsewhere (see e.g. Baker, Gleadhill and Dingle 2007; Erkkilä and Eerola 2001; Ghetti 2004; Hairo-Lax 2005; Horesh 2006a; Punkanen 2002, 2006a; Robin 2005; Ross *et al.* 2008; Ryynänen 2004; Soshensky 2001).

Music therapy in the acute phase of treatment

Drug rehabilitation can be divided into two main phases (Punkanen 2006a): (i) the acute phase, which is also called detoxification, and (ii) the follow-up phase of treatment. Follow-up phase refers here to treatment that follows detoxification and can be used in inpatient or outpatient settings, and can differ in length (Punkanen 2006a). In the acute phase of drug addiction treatment, the client's withdrawal symptoms play a central role. The starting point is in alleviating pain. Done successfully, this will help the client adhere to treatment. The central role of music therapy at this stage appears to be in helping to alleviate pain and maintaining adherence to treatment, which in other words means symptom reduction and stabilization.

In the acute phase of treatment, music therapy, that is the physioacoustic method (see Punkanen 2006b), should be used intensively, even twice a day. This should make it possible to cut down the use of benzodiazepines and painkillers, and help to create a therapeutic relationship with the client.

> When you as a therapist are able to alleviate the client's pain and bring feelings of pleasure to him through the physioacoustic method, you will get the verbal interaction from the client as a gift and the therapeutic working alliance starts to build up. (Music therapist 4)

Music therapy should be individual at this stage and the methods used should be the physioacoustic method and listening to music in the presence of the music therapist. In using the physioacoustic method, or other applications of vibroacoustic therapy (see e.g. Lehikoinen 1997; Skille and Wigram 1995; Wigram, Nygaard-Pedersen and Bonde 2002), all choices should be made according to the client's needs. The choice of treatment program depends on the client's somatic symptoms. In the acute phase of treatment, clients are usually very anxious and distressed and relaxing treatment programs should be used. The hyperaroused state of the client can best be calmed down with the use of treatment programs that have slow-paced and peaceful pulsations and fairly gentle, or weak, vibrations. We also suggest that sinusoidal sound frequencies (mostly between 30 and 80 Hz) and the duration of the treatment program should be decided according to the client's needs. Feelings of pleasure are strongly related to the use of vibroacoustic stimulus with clients in the acute phase of treatment.

> Many clients say that low frequency sound vibration feels good. I always say to them: "Do you notice that it is possible to get the experience of pleasure also without drugs?" For the client this is often the moment of insight. (Music therapist 1)

In the acute phase of treatment, the role of listening to music differs clearly from that in the follow-up phase. In the acute phase, one should avoid music that might activate images that could be associated with drug use. One should aim to support the client's feelings of relaxation and safety. When choosing music like this, it is good to consult studies on the subject of music and relaxation (see e.g. Pelletier 2004) and discuss the matter with the client. Using the physioacoustic method and listening to music offers many therapeutic possibilities in the acute phase, due to the therapist's mindful presence and an active strategy of treatment. It is the task of the therapist to bring thoughts, memories, images, emotions, and physical sensations that have arisen during vibroacoustic treatment and the listening of music into discussion, and to outline and focus the process at each session.

Music therapy in the acute phase of treatment is summarized in Table 7.1.

Table 7.1 Music therapy in the acute phase of treatment
Intensive individual therapy (even two sessions per day)
Methods: 1. physioacoustic method (or other vibroacoustic therapy application) 2. listening to music 3. therapeutic relationship
Main objectives: Alleviating pains and other withdrawal symptoms, and adhering client to treatment process

Music therapy in the follow-up phase of treatment

In the follow-up phase of treatment, music therapy should continue intensively, which could mean two or three times a week. This intensity should make process-oriented and comprehensive therapeutic work possible.

In the follow-up phase, music therapy can be individual or group therapy, or both. When moving from the acute phase to the follow-up phase of treatment, it should be noted that not all clients are able to commit to intensive individual therapy. It may take some time for the client to adjust and grow into this kind of work. On the other hand, all clients that commit to individual therapy are not capable of working in groups. It is often a good strategy to use both individual and group sessions in music therapy hand in hand. Then, for example, the issues that have arisen in individual vibroacoustic sessions can be encouraged to be taken up in the group sessions. This strategy is based on the idea that subjects and themes that in some way touch all rehabilitation clients are good to be shared also in the group, as it is then possible to hear different kinds of experiences and gain a broader perspective on them. One of the objectives of group music therapy is that it can support the social relationships between clients. One should carefully consider whether individual therapy, group therapy, or a combination of both is indicated.

There are many music therapy methods that can be used in the follow-up phase of treatment. I recommend using the physioacoustic method (or other applications of vibroacoustic therapy), listening to music, improvised or structured playing of different instruments by using the Figurenotes system (Kaikkonen 2008), singing, writing one's own songs, playing in bands, and therapeutic discussions. With these methods one can reach the client comprehensively and consider all levels of his or her experience, from sensorimotor to cognitive. It is important to keep in mind that all of these music therapy methods have to be based on a good therapeutic relationship and establishing a working alliance with the client.

The main objective of music therapy in the follow-up phase should be to uncover reasons for drug use, and on the basis of this knowledge to integrate the client's world of experiences. In uncovering reasons and motives for drug use, the central methods in music therapy are the physioacoustic method, listening to music, the mindful presence of the therapist, and therapeutic discussions. The most important thing is to be able to create conditions in which the client can open up and his or her experiences can be heard.

THREE LEVELS OF EXPERIENCE

When working at integrating the client's world of experiences, it is helpful to divide the experience into three levels: sensorimotor, emotional, and cognitive. The sensorimotor level means working with the body.

Sensorimotor processing is the capacity for processing through the body. It relies on a relatively large number of fixed action patterns like startle reflex and fight/flight responses, which often take precedence in traumatic situations. Sensorimotor processing involves sequential movement associated with movement impulses, postural changes, orienting responses, physical defensive responses, and autonomic nervous system arousal. Among the methods available in music therapy, the physioacoustic method and listening to music are very effective in evoking bodily sensations. The therapist will help the client to be more aware of his or her bodily sensations and recognize changes in sensations and behavioral impulses in different situations and in different emotional states (see e.g. Punkanen 2006b).

> We start to study with the client where and how he recognizes for example the feeling of fear in his body. Where do you feel your anger in your body? Where do you feel happiness in your body? What are the bodily sensations of different emotions? (Music therapist 1)

The emotional level of experience indicates working with a full range of feelings and encourages the expression and articulation of feeling and affect. It is also important to keep in mind that emotional processing adds motivational coloring to sensorimotor and cognitive processing. Methods that can be used in music therapy promote interaction between therapist and client, and include activities such as listening to music, playing an instrument, singing, making one's own songs, and playing in music therapy bands. The therapist will help the client to recognize and name his or her emotions, find ways to express emotions in a wider sense, and learn to regulate strong and overwhelming emotions. By using interactive emotional regulation strategies, the therapist helps the client gradually to increase his or her abilities for emotional self-regulation interactively with other people (see e.g. Schore 2003).

> When this emotional state which has been related to addictive behavior activates, you need to learn to stay with that emotion and you need to learn to find other ways to regulate and express it than using drugs, alcohol, or sex. In music therapy clients learn that all emotions belong to life. There are no right emotions and wrong emotions. The question is how you get along with different emotions and how you express them. And in this work music therapy gives a lot of possibilities. (Music therapist 1)

Cognitive processing is the capacity for conceptual cognitive information processing, reasoning, meaning-making, and decision-making. Cognitive processing necessitates the ability to observe and abstract from experience. The cognitive level of experience is connected to working with a client's thoughts, attitudes, and beliefs. First, the therapist needs to understand the significance of the client's attitudes and belief system. This means that the therapist must be able to recognize the structures of beliefs and models of attitudes that direct the client's choices and actions in everyday life and also make them visible to the client, through client–therapist interaction and dialogue. In this work, a therapist can use different kinds of belief arguments and ask the client to estimate and assess how valid or true they are to him or her. After this, the therapist can begin to challenge the client about how true those beliefs really are and question their usefulness, particularly if they interfere with rehabilitation. The client must be encouraged to study and work with his or her own beliefs through interactive action, to offer his or her experiences of achievement and capability, thus breaking the vicious circle that has maintained and strengthened the client's negative beliefs and fear of failure. Effective methods of music therapy are playing, singing, and writing one's own songs. One music therapist told me about an example of group music therapy with four men. None of the men had ever played any instruments before therapy, but by using the Figurenotes system (Finnish application of the therapy-oriented notation system; see e.g. Kaikkonen 2008) they learned to play eight songs and finally they recorded the songs with their music therapy band and made a CD with the help of the music therapist.

> They were so surprised when the CD was ready: "Hey, this is our CD! The experience that I can do things, that I have been part of something important, I play on this CD!" The feeling of success and pleasure, which is so important and different to them. (Music therapist 1)

Music therapy in the follow-up phase of treatment is summarized in Table 7.2.

Table 7.2 Music therapy in the follow-up phase of treatment
Intensive individual therapy or group therapy or combination of both (2–3 sessions per week)
Methods: 1. working with body/sensorimotor level 2. working with emotions 3. working with cognitions, attitudes, and belief system
Main objectives: Sorting out the reasons for addictive behavior, and integrating a client's levels of experience (increasing the client's integrative capacity)

Discussion

People differ from each other and there must be different methods of helping people addicted to drugs. Music therapy practice offers a lot of possibilities in drug rehabilitation, both in acute and follow-up phases of treatment. In the acute phase of treatment, music therapy can significantly strengthen and support the client's adherence to treatment. In the follow-up phase of treatment, music therapy's central role is in sorting out the reasons for addictive behavior and in integrating a client's levels of experience. With music therapy it is possible to treat the client comprehensively so that all levels of experience (sensorimotor, emotional, and cognitive) are worked on. Music therapy offers the chance for both individual and group sessions, and the range of methods available in music therapy that can be used in drug rehabilitation is wide and versatile. It is also important to remember that music is prominent in the world of drug users, so it appears to be absolutely necessary to take music into consideration in drug rehabilitation and also to process this aspect of the addiction problem.

CHAPTER 8

Gambling Addiction: Evaluation of a Multimethod Treatment Programme Including Music Therapy

Jaakko Erkkilä and Tuomas Eerola

In this chapter we focus on the experiences of a treatment programme developed in Finland in the middle of the 1990s for people with gambling addiction. Finland's Slot Machine Association (RAY), as a financier, and the Social Pedagogic Foundation, as the executor, carried out the treatment programme between 1996 and 1997. The state-controlled RAY has exclusive rights to maintain slot machines and casinos in Finland but it is also responsible for educating people about the dangers of excessive gambling, as well as for channelling resources for research and treatment, in order to reduce gambling-related problems such as gambling addiction.

The first author was invited to the project as a researcher. The aim was to produce a small-scale analysis about the functioning and benefits of the treatment programme and to write a final report on that basis. The results were finally published as a book (Erkkilä and Eerola 2001). The evaluation of the treatment programme was based on a group of clients that represented a typical, albeit small, Finnish sample (N = 27). The mean age of the participants was 36 years and their ages ranged from 25 to 66 years. However, the majority (70%) of the clients were men and a notably large number of the clients were unemployed or retired (52%). In order to concentrate on gambling addiction, an attempt was made to deselect people with multiple addictions for the treatment programme.

The whole treatment programme consisted of multiple methods, including the physioacoustic method (PhA), music listening and painting, verbal individual and group therapy and informative lectures. The role of the first author in the project was to study the whole of the treatment programme including the client experiences and the appropriateness of the methods utilised, as well as the success of the treatment in general. We focus here primarily on music therapy aspects. However, because gambling addiction is still rather a new phenomenon, both from the diagnostic and treatment point of view (DeNure 2006), the treatment model will be described in detail as well.

Gambling addiction in a nutshell

Gambling addiction is a significant public health concern and one of the most rapidly growing addictions today (Grant, Williams and Kim 2006 ; Horn 1997). Depending on the way the problem is defined, the amount of pathological gamblers has been estimated to be between 0.5 and 5.5 per cent of the population. In Finland, problem gambling and gambling addiction are above the international average (Jaakkola 2006). In DSM-IV[1] (American Psychiatric Association 1994), gambling addiction is defined as an *impulse control disorder* (see also Bondolfi *et al.* 2008). The signs of pathological gambling are varied. Like drug abusers, gamblers develop tolerance. They have to spend increasing amounts of money and take higher risks in order to get gratification (Gowen and Speyerer 1995). When a pathological gambler pays all their attention to gambling, it usually means that their life has become absorbed by gambling or by thinking about gambling. Pathological gamblers also tend to hide their problem as long as possible. It is typical that they lie to their family members or other close people about the losses and the debts (Pavalko 1999). It is not unusual that all the savings of a gambler's family are lost (Horn 1997). According to Eadington (1997), gamblers become emotionally dependent on gambling and show the signs of weakened psychosocial functioning. Pathological gamblers suffer from many psychological and physiological problems – depression, increased suicide risk, aggression (which may lead, for instance, to domestic violence), anxiousness, stress-related psychological and physiological disorders and illnesses – as well as from problems in

---

1   *Diagnostic and Statistical Manual of Mental Disorders.*

human relations (see Gowen and Speyerer 1995; Horn 1997; Kramer 1997; Pavalko 1999; Potenza 2005).

Multimethod treatment programme

Because of the variety of problems associated with gambling addiction, a multimethod approach was adopted. The treatment programme that we designed consisted of four sequential phases that lasted about one year in total (see Figure 8.1). The treatment programme was designed to have individual and group phases alternating with each other (see Table 8.1). In Phase I, the main method was physioacoustic treatment (detailed later) together with discussion with the therapist, who attempted to find out the nature and severity of the client's problem. In addition to the goals mentioned, the therapist also tried to find out whether the gambling addiction was the primary problem of the client and whether the treatment programme was suitable for them.

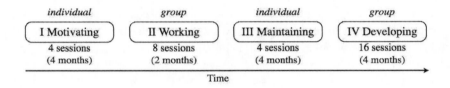

Figure 8.1 Individual and group interventions related to treatment phases over time

Phase II, which was carried out as group therapy, consists of eight sessions within a period of two months. The sessions took place once a week lasting for 180 minutes each. The main methods were group music therapy and therapeutic group discussion. Intensive working characterised this phase where the problems and solutions were of central concern. The key concepts were *rational thinking, emotion* and *training one's own will.* The aim was also to structure what had been experienced as well as to increase self-knowledge and self-discipline and to improve self-esteem.

Phase III, carried out as individual therapy, consisted of four 45-minute sessions. The sessions took place once a month so that the client had to be strong in order to avoid relapsing back into compulsive gambling. The low frequency of the sessions was intentional because the aim now was to cope with minimal support until the next, more intensive phase. Moreover, the

Table 8.1 Phases, goals and treatment methods		
Phase	**Goals**	**Treatment methods**
I MOTIVATING	Relaxation, pleasant experiences, finding a suitable group, motivation for the treatment	PhA treatment with music listening, therapeutic discussion
II WORKING	Dealing with the problem, dealing with emotions, rational thinking, finding solutions, training one's own will, working with experiences, improving self-esteem and self-knowledge	Informative lectures with discussion, therapeutic group discussion, group music therapy
III MAINTAINING	To facilitate ending of the previous phase, to motivate the client to continue the process, to get support in exploiting one's resources	PhA treatment with music listening, therapeutic discussion
IV DEVELOPING	Responsibility of the work in the group for group members, strengthening one's self, joining, consolidating what has been learned so far, coping strategies for life after treatment	Informative lectures with discussion, therapeutic group discussion, group music therapy, cultural activities

function of the less intensive phase was to allow clients to recuperate after the previous, demanding group phase.

Phase IV, carried out as group sessions, was the most intensive phase with 16 sessions in total over a period of four months. The sessions took place once a week lasting for 90 minutes each. The methods were the same as in the previous group phase but now the purpose was to give more responsibility to the group members and the ensuing processing.

Discussions, lectures and cultural activities

The programme was not exclusively based on music therapy. A multimethod approach was deemed to provide a more versatile and effective form of treatment for this group, rather than an approach relying on a single method. The other methods employed were individual and group discussions (without any musical stimuli), informative lectures, and cultural activities. One form of group discussion emphasised group processes and focused primarily on the themes that naturally arose from within the group. The group members themselves were largely responsible for the content and the therapist acted as mediator and guide in the discussion. Another form of group discussion was based on a lecture-type introduction where the lecturer/therapist aimed to activate discussion on certain, predefined themes. For instance, there were lectures where slot machine experts told about the win probabilities of the games.

Cultural activities were designed to introduce a range of cultural forms such as theatre, museums, music and so on to the clients. The aim of these activities was to obtain positive experiences and share them with the group, as well as to introduce new cultural stimulants to daily life that could replace gambling.

Physioacoustic method

The physioacoustic (PhA) method is a Finnish application, which resembles the vibroacoustic method (see Skille 1989, 1991, 1992; Wigram 1996) in many ways (see Figure 8.2). The basic idea of the method is to transmit low frequencies (27–113 Hz) to different areas of the body through the loudspeakers attached to the chair. There is a sine wave generator producing clean and easily controllable basic sound, which is amplified before being transmitted to the loudspeakers. Computer technology is employed in controlling the vibration (see Figure 8.2) and there are various predefined programmes for specific purposes, in which the frequency range, flow and location of the vibration as well as the overall intensity of the treatment can be precisely adjusted.

Physioacoustic treatment has traditionally been explained by three treatment-related effects: improving blood circulation, pain reduction and muscle relaxation. The most common contexts of the treatment are general health care, sports medicine, rehabilitation of the disabled and psychotherapy. In spite of various applying contexts, the physioacoustic method is most often connected to relaxation-related purposes. Although more research is needed, there is evidence of the positive effect of physioacoustic treatment both on physiological (blood pressure and pulse reduction) and mental (pain, tension and anxiety reduction; better concentration) domains. (Lehikoinen and Kanstren 1996; Punkanen 2006, 2007).

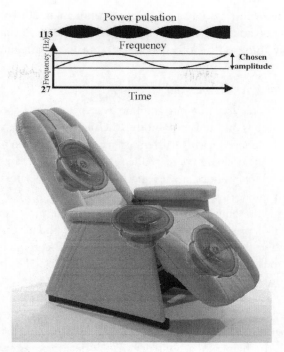

Figure 8.2 Physioacoustic chair

In the context of our treatment programme, the physioacoustic method was applied in a way that resembles what Ahonen-Eerikäinen (1996) calls the psychoauditive method, a combination based on physioacoustic treatment and music listening in order to produce bodily sensations and images. These experiences are utilised for free association where the final goal is to expand and become better aware of one's own emotions and experiences. Ahonen-Eerikäinen locates her model within psychotherapy by stating that the central aspects of the method are the flow of images, interaction between the client, music therapist and the music, and transference issues.

In our programme, the emphasis was not placed so strongly on producing images, although the therapist did not neglect such imagery if the client spontaneously produced them. We had a specific aim for the physioacoustic treatment, which was to produce a form of alternative substitute pleasure to substitute the one usually obtained from gambling. This was inspired by clinical evidence from other fields of addictions, as well as within the treatment of drug addiction in the context of music therapy, which has demonstrated the substitutional effects of physioacoustic treatment (Punkanen 2006a). Moreover, the known effects of physioacoustic treatment in reducing anxiety and tension (Punkanen 2006a), especially in the context of addiction-related problems, were also deemed to be an important, physiologically motivated addition to the treatment process.

Group music therapy: methods and rationale

Group music therapy in the programme was primarily based on music listening techniques and music painting (the method will be explained in detail later in this chapter). Music listening in a group was used for activating mental imagery. The clients were challenged to express themselves freely (free associating), to produce stories and to report their bodily experiences, associations or memories on the influence of music.

The aim of the music therapy methods in the programme was to extend the self-expression capacities of the clients and to facilitate them to get in touch with the complex emotions behind the gambling problem. The task of music is to offer an alternative tool for self-expression and communication. The most unique property of music, and art in general, are the non-verbal meanings that are difficult – or even impossible – to reach by language. When these meanings, such as complex emotional experiences with traumatic and anxious connotations, can first be attained by music with the help of symbolic distance, it becomes easier to deal with them verbally within a safe, therapeutic context. By symbolic distance we mean an indirect way to deal with difficult experiences and emotions by using symbols, metaphors, stories, and so on, instead of dealing with them directly (Erkkilä 1997a, 1997b).

Thus, some of the core ideas of the guided imagery and music (GIM) model was adopted for our treatment programme. The theoretical foundation has been explained by Goldberg (1992), whose theory on the effect of music in triggering emotions and producing images is based on research on memory functions and mechanisms (see also Plutchik 1984). In this work, a connection between emotions and images has been established. When we experience an emotion, it tends to trigger an image attached to that emotion. According to Goldberg, all the images in our memory are more or less emotional. We can then conclude that the images that spring up in our mind are not random but appear to be linked with certain stimuli. For instance, an object that once belonged to someone who has been very important for us, but who has passed away, may generate a strong, emotional image of its original owner. Through associative memory one image triggers another, the second the third, and so on. This process may lead to an intensive moment where one remembers the person who has passed away. What often happens is that during these moments one can recall something that has been in limbo for a long time.

It is known that music is an extremely potent media for triggering emotions (see Juslin and Västfjäll 2008). However, most often we do not interpret the emotions as such but prefer recalling the images that the music has evoked. Following Goldberg's theoretical framework, we can conclude that when, there are images, there must also be emotions in the background. In sum, Goldberg (1992) describes listening to the music as a cycle where music first creates an emotional context consisting of various dynamic movements/forms. Any such musical passage or movement (M) can trigger an emotion (E), which then triggers an image (I). Through associative memory functions one image can lead to another and so on. Thus, music listening and ensuing imagery can be described as cycles such as M–E–I–I–I–M–E–I and so on.

However, these chains of associations may not be totally arbitrary in music. The 'trick' of the music is that there is always a certain emotional context in a composition. Hence, the listener does not have total freedom when the musical movements do arise from certain, usually coherent emotional contexts. This way the music may 'force' the listener towards certain emotional qualities and contexts and this property probably has a significant role in the intensity and profoundness of the experiences, emotions and images generated by the music.

In summary, the idea of music listening in the treatment programme was the following:

1. To produce experiences such as emotional imagery that are connected to the participant's addiction.
2. To create a safe and confidential context where the music-related experiences can be elaborated and explored more fully, allowing the participant to deal with the most anxious, painful, even paradoxical contents attached to imagery, emotions and the experiences.
3. To offer a participant the possibility of sharing what has been experienced with the other group members, and to obtain meaningful insights into these experiences.
4. To shed light on the gambling addiction in general via individual and group experiences and hence to help the participants to get insights – not only by dealing with one's own problems but by learning from others as well.

Physiological measures, self-ratings, questionnaires and drawings

To provide measures of the relaxation and subjective feelings of anxiety, stress and tiredness data were collected before and after group sessions. As the aim of the project was mainly to establish and execute a treatment programme for gambling addiction, less effort was allocated for research purposes. Thus, we had to develop an economic way to get the data we needed for the analysis. A number of questionnaires were administered both before and after the sessions (clients), or only after the sessions (therapists). These questionnaires had to be quick to complete so that they would not take too much time away from the treatment. In PhA treatment it was possible to use blood pressure measures for getting basic physiological data in order to evaluate the relaxation effect of the sessions. In addition, the music therapists were asked to collect all the paintings from the music painting sessions. All the therapists were offered an opportunity to keep a therapist's diary where they wrote freely about the most important themes and phenomena in the sessions based on their own experiences.

Evaluation of the multimethod treatment programme

The following summarises the results of the treatment programme by starting from the possible reductions in the frequency of gambling and then moving towards various other indicators of the coming to terms with the addiction during the individual and group sessions.

Gambling frequency, moods and the commitment to the therapy

A central question is, of course, whether the treatment programme helps the participants to stop gambling or enable them to regain control of their behaviour. The participants had to report the frequency of gambling between each of the sessions (see Figure 8.3). The numbers on the x-axis indicate the frequency of gambling where 0 = 'not at all', 1 = 'once between the sessions', 2 = 'twice between the sessions', 3 = 'three times between the sessions' and 4 = '4 or more', and the y-axis is the proportion of the clients (N # = # 27). It is evident that the amount of gambling gradually decreases, and in the final phase there is a significant number of clients who do not gamble at all. Despite this trend, a few clients still gambled considerably at the end of the treatment programme. Relapses were also common so that the non-gamblers' group (those who are not currently gambling) did not consist of the same people during the treatment process.

Some participants also tested their 'condition' by gambling every now and then in a controlled way.

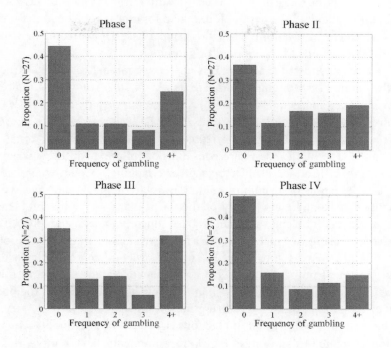

Figure 8.3 Frequency of gambling in each phase of treatment

Another interesting question is the commitment to the treatment. The whole treatment programme lasted a minimum of one year and required the clients to be committed between the sessions and phases without any external support. A simple way to assess the commitment to treatment is to look at the amount of absence in the sessions. In individual phases I and III, the attendance was 100 per cent because the sessions were agreed individually with each client. In group phases II (8 sessions) and IV (16 sessions), attendance was based on the clients' own motivation and therefore reveals individual commitment to the treatment programme. The attendance in the two group phases was 77 per cent (Phase II) and 60 per cent (Phase IV). There was a trend that, towards the end of the phases, attendance decreased, in particular in Phase IV (longer group phase). A higher attendance in the first group phase may stem from the fact that it was shorter than the second group phase. However, because the overall absence rate was rather high in the latter phase, we were interested in knowing whether other reasons for that phenomenon could be found. For example, if one has obtained help and has been able to avoid gambling for a long time, this might be a reason for not being motivated to attend the sessions. On the other hand, if one has not found help for one's problem, it may also affect treatment motivation. With the group Phase IV, we compared the order of the sessions to the amount of gambling.

The analysis showed that there was no connection between the absence and the amount of gambling chi-square test ($\chi^2 = 10.22$, $df = 16$, $p = .86$).[2] Only substance abuse (mostly alcohol) could explain weakly the increase of absences towards the end of the group Phase IV (*Spearman's rank correlation coefficient, r = −0.19, df = 229, p < 0.005*).[3]

In summary, the questionnaire data did not fully explain the absences from the group. There are likely to be many overlapping reasons for absences, such as the nature of gambling addiction as a complex syndrome with difficulties in commitment. Many of the participants had other problems such as mental problems, substance abuse, unemployment and problems with human relations, which may have a role in overall treatment motivation. There might be a reason to revise the overall structure and content details of the treatment programme as well. For instance, readjusting the lengths of the phases and considering boosting the motivational aspects of the final parts of the group phases might bring improvements.

The analysis also revealed interactions between different mood ratings, amount of gambling and physiological measurements. For example, those who were classified as 'high-gamblers' evaluated their moods consistently more negatively than those who were 'low-gamblers'. An overall summary of the relationship between the mood and amount of gambling over time is portrayed in Figure 8.4.

The y-axis, in Figure 8.4, is the proportion of negative adjectives the clients reported and the x-axis is the amount of gambling. The mood ratings were obtained from a questionnaire, where the clients could choose, from an array of 20 adjectives, the ones that corresponded with their mood (half of these adjectives were negative and half positive and resembled the PANAS-X mood questionnaire in many respects; see Watson, Clark

---

2   The chi-square test is a measure of association between two distributions consisting of nominal categories. The p-value relating to the test statistic indicates the probability of this association assuming that the null hypothesis is true.

3   Rank correlations that measure the association between two rankings are useful when the items compared are not distributed according to a normal distribution or the distances between the scales within the item are not known. The output of the correlations are from −1 (perfect negative association), to 0 (no association) and to 1 (perfect association; that is, the two rankings are identical) and the p-value relates this ranking to a null hypothesis.

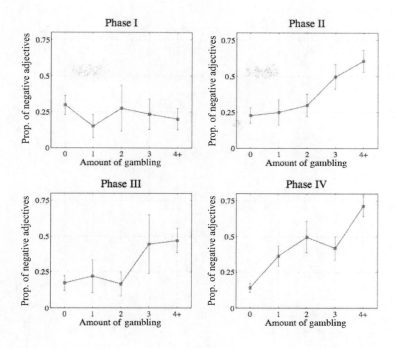

Figure 8.4. Relationship between mood (negative adjectives) and amount of gambling over time

and Tellegen 1988). In the analysis, the adjectives were categorised into positive and negative and used as an overall indication of the mood (see Figure 8.4). To investigate the psychological states of the participants in more detail, self-report measures of anxiety and psychological stress using Visual Analogue Scales (VAS; 0–50) were collected separately before and after each session (see Figure 8.5). In Figure 8.5 we see that the gambling problem is related to psychological stress. It is interesting that in Phase I, when the treatment process was at the beginning, a high amount of gambling seemed not to be related to negative moods. When the 'real work' of therapy and the treatment starts from Phase II (which was the first group phase), a high amount of gambling is already associated with negative moods. The adjectives chosen then were, for instance, 'guilt', 'anxiety' and 'shame'. This pattern suggests that the treatment programme made the clients well aware of their problem, which is vital for the success of the treatment.

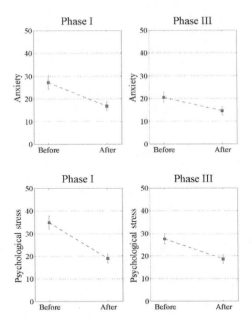

Figure 8.5 Phases of treatment, changes in anxiety and changes in psychological stress. The error bars display standard errors

Individual phases and the physiological and self-report measures

Phases I and III consisted of PhA treatment and therapeutic discussion. Earlier studies have found a connection between stress-related problems and pathological gambling (Pavalko 1999). Thus, it was interesting to investigate whether a combination consisting of PhA treatment and therapeutic discussion would help the clients to relax and to decrease the prevalent negative moods associated with the problem.

Blood pressure and heart rate measurements, as well as subjective self-assessments, showed decrease in self-reported (Figure 8.5) and physiologically measured (Figure 8.6) stress indicators during the course of the session. There is a relationship between blood pressure, anxiety and stress, and indeed blood pressure has been used as an indicator of improved stress management and relaxation (Crowther 1983; Peters, Benson and Peters 1977; Rainforth *et al.* 2007).

Figure 8.5 displays the clients' estimations of their psychological well-being given at the beginning of the session and at the end of the same

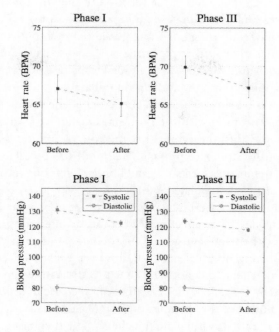

Figure 8.6 Changes in heart rate and blood pressure related to treatment phases. The error bars display standard errors

session. The differences in all these questions were large and statistically significant (*repeated ANOVA, F = 8.23 and F = 4.19, p < 0.01 and p < 0.05, for Phases I and III for anxiety; F = 20.27 and F = 9.00, p < 0.01, for Phases I and III for psychological stress*). The physiological measurements (pulse and blood pressure) were in line with self-reports, albeit the changes were not as clear (Figure 8.6).

Although the pattern of the physiological results resembles those obtained from the self-reports, there were factors such as age, gender and physical fitness that could not be controlled thoroughly (due to a limited number of participants in this study). Any conclusions about physiological changes caused by the treatment clearly warrant further investigation.

Group music therapy and the role of creative imagery, discussion and drawings

Music had different goals in individual and group phases. In the individual phases, music was primarily used for relaxation and activating pleasant experiences. In the group phases, the function of the music was to activate mental processes and to facilitate emotional expression. In other words, the role of music was to bring (emotional) material from pre-consciousness into consciousness to be further processed and analysed, and interpreted in a verbal domain. Music therapy was designed to be one of several methods and not to be applied throughout the group phase.

The questionnaires showed that the clients experienced the music mainly as a useful tool in coping with the problem. Qualitative analysis revealed more details about this, indicating that the role of music was important in dealing with the strong emotions linked with the problem, as well as describing the traumatic aspects of gambling by symbolic means (images, paintings, stories, etc.) stimulated by the music. Moreover, music tended to stimulate and deepen the discussion in some sessions where discussion seemed to be trifling or troublesome. There is an interesting example of this with one of the treatment groups. In the middle of Phase IV none of the clients gambled. This ideal situation, however, caused a decrease in the intensity and the clients did not have much to discuss: 'when there is no problem, there is not much to discuss either'. A decrease in overall intensity and dynamics bothered the therapist and he decided to start using music listening again in order to stimulate the clients. The therapist reported that in this way the group was able to restore the intensity.

Music therapists frequently used different kinds of instructions when engaging the clients in imagery processes with music. This is demonstrated in a following quotation from an instruction given by a therapist:

> Let the music take you to a time, to a place somewhere, as you wish. Imagine now a path and you are walking that path. Sometimes you walk faster, sometimes slower. You may stop for a while to look at the landscape. You may meet somebody on the path. Make a mental note what you see and experience during your trip. You can draw or write about your experiences.

Usually the therapist customised the topics around the particular, topical themes of the group. As an overall finding, we found that the clients in all groups seemed to respond favourably and naturally and were receptive to the combination of creative imagery, music and discussions. Also a music-painting method was employed. This consisted of a three-stage process, where symbolic contents, yet without conscious meanings, were gradually brought into the domain of conscious thinking:

1. *Focusing on one's own mental contents with music and guided by the therapist.*
    In this, the mind is first allowed to wander freely without any

concrete anchor point. Gradually something more concrete, such as single words, a feeling, a colour, a symbol, emerge from the free associational flow.

2. *Creating a painting where the still fragmented mental contents are spontaneously transferred onto paper.* The products of this process may still be rather abstract but sometimes they might be clearly representational as well. This stage externalises, or makes visible, what was first internal and invisible.

3. *Discussion based on the imagery process.* The 'passengers' talk about their experiences and discuss the meanings of the creative output with the group. This way various, sometimes shareable, motives, emotions and many other phenomena behind the addiction can be detected and recognised.

In the following, excerpts from the data illustrate how the clients processed their problem in the music-painting context.

Crossroads symbolism is apparent in Figure 8.7, which outlines the two alternatives. If the client is able to end the gambling and stay away from it, a new car, a sailing boat, a summerhouse may be available to him. If the client is not (and takes the lower road), the final outcome is distressing: only gambling, or death.

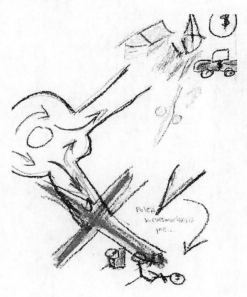

Figure 8.7 'Crossroads' symbolism in a client's painting

In Figure 8.8, we find a polarity resembling the interpretation found in the previous drawing (Figure 8.7). The blind alley on the left seems to be full of anxious themes. The wall has been inscribed with the names of typical Finnish money games together with the words 'must', 'despair', 'sweat', 'rush' and so on. On the right side of the picture, the sun is shining and the caption in the bubble declares 'friends', 'close people', 'work', 'balance' and 'joy' – all of which will not be reachable or enjoyable if one continues gambling.

By means of music the clients were able to create images associated with the problem. An example of this is given in the following quotation, which is a client's statement after guided image travel with music:

> I was disappointed when you [the therapist] said at the end that we should come back on the shore where we started the journey from. There, on the other side of the water, I would have had a new future. It would have been another one – without any opportunities for gambling.

In summary, the group sessions combined discussions and various creative efforts (music listening, drawings) to activate the mental processes and emotional expression connected with the problem behaviour. It was found that music and drawings were both effective in bringing emotional material from the pre-conscious to conscious.

Figure 8.8 Images associated with anxiety in a client's painting

Discussion

Addiction problems have often been treated in group settings (Gamblers Anonymous, for example). Our project also brought out that being able to share the problem with others with the same problem is of great importance. The two individual phases were important too, but had different functions. Phase I was the selection, orientation and assessment for the later programme. Phase III offered a break between the two group phases by supporting a client's motivation to complete the programme. However, during Phase III, many clients commented that they missed the group sessions and looked forward to meeting their group members again. This is a clear indication for us about the importance of the group for the clients.

The multimethod approach of the treatment programme probably had its role in maintaining the treatment motivation. However, it is difficult to say what the reason was for fading intensity of the group in Phase IV. There were probably several reasons. Maybe the phase was too long, or the group members had too much responsibility for the content.

One of the principles of the programme was that the therapist should be an equal group member whose role was to encourage open communication within the group. Sometimes this principle worked well but, in periods when the intensity of communication decreases, it might be a good idea for the therapist to adopt a more active or directive role. There might also be room for developing the interaction between the clinical methods such as group music therapy versus verbal group therapy. Finally, the clinical population in question probably was rather challenging from a motivational point of view, which had to be taken into account as well.

There are various theories about the reasons for developing gambling addiction. This programme brought out that many clients had complex problems in their personal biographies, such as a broken home, traumatic experiences both in childhood and in later life, as well as untreated psychiatric problems. On one hand, 'psychodynamic' explanation stresses the various individual reasons behind the gambling addiction. This fits nicely with Pavalko's (1999) concept of 'escape gambler', where one gambles to escape their personal problems. On the other hand, there were participants in this study who seemed to have inherited an addiction problem. They may have close relatives with addictions – most often alcoholism. They also discussed their innate weaknesses during the treatment. This observation supports Eisen's (1998) notion about the role of genetics, which should be taken into account when searching for answers to gambling addiction. Genetically mediated variations of dopaminergic subsystems and resulting altered reward functions may be a link to an individual susceptibility and vulnerability to addictive behaviours (Yacubian and Büchel 2009). We found also 'action seeker' (Pavalko 1999; Stoil and Blaszczynski 1994) gamblers where one gambles for the arousal it gives, and those who gambled to ease the feelings of loneliness and frustration (see Moran 1970). In sum, planning and carrying out a treatment programme for people with gambling addiction is challenging because there are various reasons why an individual has become a compulsive gambler. It seems that the treatment methods used should relate to the primary cause for gambling. Our decision to use a multimethod treatment approach in the project served this purpose and allowed us to obtain experience of various methods. The experiences and the feedback from using a range of methods was mostly positive and highlighted how methodological variability may help to increase the motivation of clients and provide alternative ways of addressing the problem.

Summary of gambling addiction

- Gambling is an illness of addiction and more effort should be addressed towards accurate diagnosis.
- Other addictions, such as substance abuse, easily conceal the gambling addiction. Thus, when treating an addiction, attention should be given to possible cross-addiction issues.
- Gambling addiction develops gradually. Thus, more attention should be paid to adolescents' gambling behaviour as well as to preventive activities.
- People with difficulties in resisting different kinds of temptations are at risk of developing gambling addiction.
- Severe psychiatric disorders, in particular depression, psychosomatic illnesses and suicidal thinking and suicide attempts, are common in people with gambling addiction.
- The prevalence of gambling addiction increases with the availability and accessibility of new applications such as online gaming and because of liberalism in regulation policy. When gambling addiction becomes more prevalent, then the negative side-effects, such as criminal activities and domestic violence, also increase.

Recommendations for the treatment of gambling addiction

- It may be reasonable to divide a long treatment programme into sub-periods with different goals and methods. Employing both individual and group settings within the overall programme was beneficial for the treatment.
- Attention should be paid to the length of the group phases and the role of the therapist within these. We found that intensity typically decreased after six to eight group sessions, after which a more directive role for the therapist, or a more intensive way of working, is probably necessary.
- Cognitive and psychodynamic approaches were included in the treatment programme, a combination which seemed to result in a complementary as well as a rather positive working basis for the treatment of adults with gambling addiction.
- The multimethod treatment programme is a fruitful approach with this group but more attention should be addressed to the location, interaction of the different methods, as well as to the internal coherence of the phases within the programme.
- The music therapy methods employed in the treatment programme support and complement the overall programme at least in the following areas: mental and physiological relaxation, compensatory pleasure, dealing with the problem through images, metaphors, associations and symbols, and dealing with emotions linked with the problem.
- The participants of the programme consisted of adults. For adolescents, a more action-directed, functional approach would probably work better.

CHAPTER 9

The Aldridge Model: An Ecological Systemic Approach

David Aldridge

On the spectrum of deviant and extreme behaviour, the phenomenon of addictive behaviour is one of the least accessible. Understanding this phenomenon, and finding ways of addressing the problems it presents, is complex and difficult. As we have seen earlier, behaviour defined as deviant is based upon the context in which the behaviour occurs. Extreme forms of behaviour, like suicidal behaviour and extreme child distress, are embedded in a wide social, cultural and political context of place and time and are the cumulative results of an escalating process of attempted distress resolution or problem-solving (Aldridge 1998; Avraham-Krehwinkel and Aldridge 2009). Instead of regarding the phenomenon of addiction as a personality disorder or a fixed pattern of deviance located in the individual, we can see addictive behaviours as a cyclical pattern of escalating interactions. This provides us with an understanding of social reality on a wider time-scale, offering a perspective of circular causality (see Figure 9.1) where self-medication becomes a strategy of distress management. The distress itself is located within the ecology of people living their lives together but expressed by one person. However, self-medication may become a legitimised strategy that is colluded with when distress is not resolved.

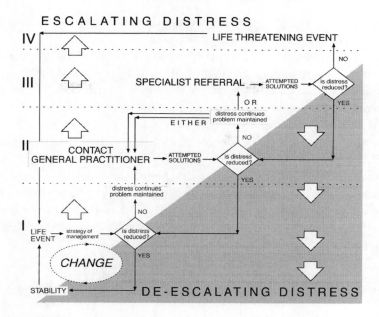

Figure 9.1 Change, attempted solutions and cycles of escalating and de-escalating distress

New alternatives emerge out of this approach. Their main advantage lies in redefining maladaptive delinquent acts into acts of attempted problem resolution thereby enhancing change. Such an approach enables the reframing of senseless acts of personal inadequacy to meaningful acts of social significance, thus promoting change and conflict resolution. If we consider ourselves not as junkies or drinkers, and escape the role of deviant victims, then we can also consider ourselves as simple human beings struggling to cope with life's challenges alongside those who are nearest and dearest to us.

Addiction can be seen as a description of the way in which the systemic behaviour is organised to relieve distress. This view enables us to negotiate addictive behaviours through a shared focused effort of all participants in a given situation.

The shift in focus here has further implications, mainly on the goal of therapy. Therapy does not seek to fix what went wrong or to accommodate pathology and deviance – it enables the beginning of a process of change by referring to competence and resources. All efforts of all participants join to negotiate the same means and attain the same goal. Based on the effort to understand the rules, beliefs and language of the family, the therapist plays the role of a facilitator, offering choices and making them available to the family. Family boundaries not only provide the individual with his identity but they also serve to constrain his behaviour.

The wider perspective of the eco-systemic approach has its focus not only on the deviant individual and his behaviour, but on the whole complex of significant others and the different systems in which he operates. The emphasis on the collective, as well as the shift from feeling to action, is central to this alternative view of deviant and extreme behaviour where the person is located within close relationships that are themselves located within a larger context of community.

What is essential for any positive change to relieve distress is a flexible repertoire of distress management. The problem with addictive behaviours is that substance abuse is a 'one size fits all' solution. Or for drinkers, one solution, alcohol, fits all sizes of problem as a limited repertoire of distress management.

A model of the systemic management of distress

> Stabilization of relationship has been called the 'rule of the relationship' and works in the interest of economy (it leaves many behaviours from the repertoire to be used no longer). (Jackson 1965, p.6)

This perspective provides a repertoire of behaviours for the management of distress in families. These behaviours are at once individual and collective, personal and social. They are also seen as either legitimate or illegitimate by individuals within the family, by the family itself and by their social context. Thus, particular personal behaviours may be legitimate to one person but illegitimate to others.

Challenging behaviour, like substance abuse, is seen from this perspective as a strategy for controlling change and coping with distress within the family group. Family or small groups are stressed by developmental or lifecycle changes where substances may be used to reduce, manage or avoid conflict. Challenging behaviour is a communicative process expressing a challenging situation that reflects the family system as a whole and is an attempt to manage the rate of change in a family. Therefore, challenging behaviour is a social phenomenon. Families organise themselves to manage developmental crises in varying ways. Some families accommodate change easily and naturally without excess levels of distress. Some families develop within their own cultural tradition a means of accommodating change that involves hostility and conflict leading to high levels of distress. In some families, familial distress is managed by one family member becoming deviant. Indeed, some families use substances quite legitimately as a means of regulating distress.

We have an armamentarium of psychoactive substances, culturally validated and professionally prescribed for that purpose. We have subcultures and economies organised around the consumption of alcohol and other substances. However, at some point one person acts as a material cause representing distress at a different systemic level of interaction that becomes seen as deviant or abnormal. What we need to consider is that the individual represents a pattern of social transactions.

My model proposes a general model for understanding the systemic management of distress. This model understands systemic distress at different levels of organisation: individual, familial or cultural (see Figures 9.1 and 9.2). Although conceived of as a circular process it will be necessary for the purpose of description to interrupt this circularity and begin at one point – we have to start somewhere. The point chosen to start this cycle is that of a system facing a crisis. I am assuming here that any dynamic system is constantly scrutinising itself as to its current status to maintain stability.

In Figure 9.2 we see that a developmental crisis is recognised (a) by a system according to its own construings, that are in turn located within and informed by a cultural context. Something happens. A life event occurs. This event can be a change in blood pressure, the entrance of a virus to the system, a personal disappointment or an argument with a partner. Something happens that constitutes an 'event', the consequences of which must be resolved.

As an adaptation to that event, thresholds of distress are threatened (b) (see Section X in Figure 9.2). Someone is upset.

There then follows a strategic move to reduce that distress according to the repertoire of distress management that the individual has (c). Blood pressure may be regulated by sitting down and relaxing, the immune system may react to the virus, we may cry in frustration or retire to a quiet place. We may take a pill or imbibe a drink. Distress is reduced (d). What has happened is regulated successfully within the terms of the system itself. The repertoire for relieving distress is validated (e), it works and stability is maintained (f). This is a simple homeostatic loop as we see in Section X of Figure 9.2.

However, should distress not be reduced then an alternative strategy from the repertoire of distress management is used, and the system scrutinises itself for levels of distress. We may reduce blood pressure by meditating, we can wait for a head cold to come and go or a child may run around boisterously and shout. Maybe we take pills over a longer period of time or

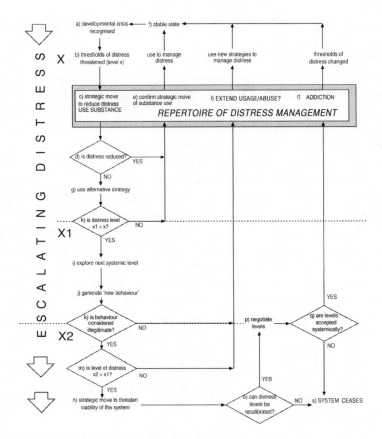

Figure 9.2 Levels of escalating distress and systemic strategies of management

an extra glass of alcohol. If distress is reduced then this alternative strategy (g) is validated as a legitimate means of reducing distress. This also explains why substance abuse may run in families without necessarily having a genetic origin. It is simply an acceptable strategy in the repertoire of distress management that is learned. Tolerance is not simply a physiological phenomenon for the individual but also a systemic phenomenon within a family or social group.

If distress continues to escalate (h) where levels of distress are higher than in Section X, and systemic thresholds are threatened to excess to a point where the very viability of the system itself is threatened, then distress management strategies are explored from a higher level of systemic organisation, stage (i) in Section X1. A shift occurs from the organic to the personal, or from personal to marital, marital to familial, familial to communal, communal to social, or departmental to organisational.

This strategy will depend upon the systemic rules for distress management at this contextual level and will accord to the tradition of the system, that is the biography, memory and construing of the system. In this way 'new' behaviour to the individual is generated (j). Patients suffering emotional distress in contact with the psychiatric service are introduced to new ways of expressing that distress. Children and parents may learn from grandparents, social workers may suggest alternatives, religious elders may offer counselling. Drinkers may find other substances to abuse or different venues to frequent.

If this behaviour is considered legitimate (k) then it effectively extends the repertoire of distress management (l). Distress repertoires are extended by being informed within a cultural matrix. We learn about the most sympathetic general practitioner, alternative medical practices, lay healing practices, differing psychotherapeutic techniques, the latest diets, exercises and alternative lifestyles to alleviate distress. It must be noted here that the current level of distress may be higher than at (b) although still within the thresholds of tolerable distress. In this way, some systems live with raised levels of distress: learning to live with pain, anxiety, depression and delinquency. Indeed, some families live with a high level of conflict tolerance that may become accepted as everyday life. Some people live with drinking patterns that would be unacceptable to others but are acceptable to their partners. While there are governmental guidelines about how many units of alcohol can be safely consumed each week, these 'social' thresholds may be regularly transgressed.

Current levels of distress may not fall to the initial levels (m). The system then calibrates itself to accommodate a higher level of distress. Distress at X2 is still greater than at X. When this occurs a family with a child who becomes symptomatic to maintain the family stability may become a family system with a necessarily symptomatic member, for example diabetic, asthmatic, problematic, anorectic, epileptic, tense, depressed, delinquent or alcoholic. Not only is the repertoire of distress management extended (l) but the initial thresholds of distress (b) are altered. The system returns itself to a stable state (f), but that state is altered. Distress is endemic to the family system and becomes a way of relating. Perhaps more significantly, physiological tolerance is so altered within the individual that physical addiction occurs.

If distress levels escalate such that systemic viability is further threatened, then an overt strategic move is made to threaten the viability of the system (n). This move will be one which is culturally approved and based upon the systemic tradition of manifesting distress, for example blood sugar levels escalate into diabetes and then diabetic coma, essential hypertension becomes raised and develops into a stroke, delinquent behaviours escalate into challenging episodes of physical contact and abuse or strategies of medication escalate into self-poisoning or alcoholic coma.

When a system becomes so threatened it will be necessary to implement measures to reduce distress and maintain systemic viability (o). This will be observed in those behavioural strategies used in a crisis. The vital question is, can thresholds of distress be recalibrated? For some physiological levels this may not be physically possible and the patient dies. For some psychological levels, this calibration may mean a continuing psychotic episode or perceptual outbursts of anger. For some social situations there is withdrawal, hospitalisation and temporary estrangement.

Should these crisis strategies fail and the systemic thresholds are exceeded then the system will cease (s). Someone dies, leaves or is forcibly removed.

On the other hand, a crisis may successfully be negotiated (p) and an attempt is made to recalibrate the systemic thresholds of distress and change systemic construing (q). Thresholds of distress are then changed within the repertoire of distress management (r). Should the negotiation of such systemic change not be successfully validated throughout the system to the satisfaction of all members then the system will cease (s). In this way we see that people leave families by death, leave marriages by divorce, become expelled from school, sacked from an organisation and discharged from hostels. At the organic level, livers are ruined or brains damaged.

In this model, using a substance can be seen as a means of promoting change and maintaining stability. But substance use may also promote further conflict, and levels of distress are tolerated at a level higher than the initial level. Substance use becomes seen as abuse and itself becomes a life event threatening stability. Throughout this model, strategic moves that attempt to reduce distress and recalibrate the system may themselves act reflexively as 'life events', which in their turn have to be accommodated. Having a drink or taking a pill becomes the problem. This is the process of iatrogenesis, where treatment can also be a cause of further problems. We see this when pain medication becomes substance abuse.

The Contributors

Reza Abdollahnejad is a psychologist and music therapist from Tehran, Iran. He works as a researcher and therapist in the field of addiction and substance abuse. He is the director of Tehran Therapeutic Community, and established the first Iranian Therapeutic Community Association. In addition, he established a music therapy program in the Tehran Therapeutic Community and has trained many psychologists, social workers and psychiatrists in the application of music therapy for the treatment of substance abuse, especially in residential settings.

David Aldridge, PhD., FRSM. is Co-Director of the Nordoff-Robbins Zentrum in Witten, Germany. He has published widely in the field of music therapy and in health care delivery. His recent work based on international co-operations concentrates on offering guidance to families and professionals where there are difficulties with children and adolescents. These titles include: "A Non-Violent Resistance Approach with Children in Distress: A Guide for Parents and Professionals" Jessica Kingsley 2010 with Carmelite Avraham-Krehwinkel, Israel and a forthcoming sequel to his book about suicide in families, "Understanding suicide: A guide for the Family and the Professional" with Sergio Perez, Cuba. He is also active in an international scientific network concerned with the field of genetics, developmental delay and early intervention. This work will appear as "Fragile X Syndrome: A guide for Families and Professionals" with Isabel Fernandez Carvajal, Spain.

Irene Dijkstra, BA, SRMTh (senior registered music therapist) works in a private and public addiction clinic as administrator and as music therapist. She is a member of the Dutch Training Advisory Committee for addiction and freelance lecturer at the MIAM (Masters in Addiction Medicine)

Tuomas Eerola, (PhD, Senior Researcher) is Senior Researcher at the Finnish Centre of Excellence in Interdisciplinary Music Research within the University of Jyväskylä, Finland. His research interest lies within the field of music cognition and music psychology, currently mainly in perception and induction of emotions in music..

Jaakko Erkkila, PhD, is a Professor of Music Therapy and head of the Department of Music, University of Jyvaskyla (UJy), Finland. He is the head of studies of music therapy master's programme (UJy) and of music therapy clinical studies in Eino Roiha Institute, Jyväskylä. Erkkilä is the vice president of the European Music Therapy Confederation. His research activities include themes such as improvisational music psychotherapy in general, microanalysis of music therapy actions and processes, and randomised controlled trials in music therapy contexts.

Jörg Fachner, Dr. rer. med. research interests include music therapy and its applications in healing cultures, modern medicine and special education; on the social pharmacology of music; on music and the reward system in the brain; and on popular music culture and performance. He has published "Music and altered states" with David Aldridge for Jessica Kingsley Publishers in 2006. His current research at University of Jyväskylä in Finland focuses on music perception in depressive and stroke states realised with a QEEG paradigm.

Ted Ficken, Ph.D., MT-BC, CPHQ is a Music Therapist-Board Certified (MT-BC), and a Certified Professional in Healthcare Quality (CPHQ), working as the Director of Quality Improvement at Oregon State Hospital in Salem, Oregon. He has served as an adjunct faculty member in the music therapy program at Marylhurst University in Portland, Oregon, and in the health care administration program at Oregon State University, in Corvallis, Oregon.

Laurien Hakvoort, MA, SRMTh works as researcher on her PhD in forensic psychiatry (FPC Oostvaarderskliniek) and teaches music therapy methodology at ArtEZ Conservatory of Music. She also has a private practice, Muzis, as a music therapist www.muzis.net.

John P. Hedigan (RMT, MMus) is an Australian music therapist who has worked extensively with substance dependent adults, within the Therapeutic Community model. He currently works at the Austin Hospital in Melbourne, specialising in psychiatry and palliative care.

Tsvia Horesh (MA, RMT) was born in the U.S.A. and grew up in Israel. She is a member of Psychoactive - Mental Health Professionals for Human Rights, and is involved in mental health projects relating to the Israeli-Palistenean conflict. Ms. Horesh has published papers and lectured on related subjects at music therapy congresses in Israel, Italy, England, Canada and Holland.

Marko Punkanen is a social educator, music therapist, dance/movement therapist and trauma psychotherapist, working in a private practice in Lahti, Finland. His special interest is how traumatic background affects and is related to addiction behaviour. Currently he also works as a researcher at the Finnish Centre of Excellence in Interdisciplinary Music Research, University of Jyväskylä.

References

Abler, B., Erk, S. and Walter, H. (2005) 'The human reward system – Insights from neuroimaging and clinical implications.' *Nervenheilkunde 24*, 3, 1–8.

Ahlström, S. (1998) 'Sosiokulttuurinen tausta ja juomatavat' ['Sociocultural background and drinking habits']. In M. Salaspuro, K. Kiianmaa and K. Seppä (eds) *Päihdelääketiede*, 20–28. Jyväskylä: Gummerus.

Ahonen-Eerikäinen, H. (1996) 'Psykoauditiivinen musiikkiterapiamenetelmä' [Psychoauditive method for music therapy'] *Musiikkiterapia 1*, 33–45.

Ainsworth, M., Belhar, M., Waters, E. and Wall, S. (1978) *Patterns of Attachment: A Psychological Study of the Strange Situation*. Hillsdale, NJ: Erlbaum.

Aldridge, D. (1984) 'Suicidal behaviour and family interaction.' *Journal of Family Therapy 6*, 309–322.

Aldridge, D. (1989) 'A phenomenological comparison of the organization of music and the self'. *Arts in Psychotherapy 16*, 91–97.

Aldridge, D. (1994) 'Alzheimer's Disease: Rhythm, timimg and music as therapy.' *Biomedicine and Pharmacotherapy 48*, 7, 275–281.

Aldridge, D. (1998) *Suicide: The Tragedy of Hopelessness*. London: Jessica Kingsley Publishers.

Aldridge, D. and Fachner, J. (eds) (2006) *Music and Altered States – Consciousness, Transcendence, Therapy and Addictions*. London: Jessica Kingsley Publishers.

Aldridge, G., and Aldridge, D. (2008) *Melody in Music Therapy: A Therapeutic Narrative Analysis*. London: Jessica Kingsley Publishers.

American Psychiatric Association (1994) *Diagnostic and Statistical Manual of Mental Disorders – DSM-IV*. Washington, DC: American Psychiatric Association.

Amir, D. (1990) 'A song is born: Discovering meaning in improvised songs through a phenomenological analysis of two music therapy sessions with a traumatic spinal cord injured young adult.' *Music Therapy 9*, 1, 62–81.

Appelbaum, A.H. (1996) 'Why traumatized borderline patients relapse.' *Bulletin of the Menninger Clinic 60*, 4, 449–463.

Avraham-Krehwinkel, C. and Aldridge, D. (2009) *A Non-Violent Resistance Approach to Children in Distress: A Guide for Parents and Practitioners*. London: Jessica Kingsley Publishers.

Baker, F.A., Gleadhill, L.M. and Dingle, G.A. (2007) 'Music therapy and emotional exploration: Exposing substance abuse clients to the experiences of non-drug-induced emotions.' *The Arts in Psychotherapy 34*, 4, 321–330.

Bateson, G. (1973) *Steps to an Ecology of Mind*. London: Granada.

Battisti, M.C., Noto, A.R., Nappo, S. and Carlini Ede, A. (2006) 'A profile of Ecstasy (MDMA) use in Sao Paulo, Brazil: An ethnographic study.' *Journal of Psychoactive Drugs 38*, 1, 13–18.

Baudelaire, C. (1994) *Artificial Paradises*. Secaucus, NJ: Carol Publishing Group.

Becker, H.S. (1963) *Outsiders: Studies in the Sociology of Deviance*. New York: Free Press.

Becker-Blease, K.A. (2004) 'Dissociative states through new age and electronic trance music.' *Journal of Trauma & Dissociation 5*, 2, 89–100.

Bednarz, L.F. and Nikkel, B. (1992) 'The role of music therapy in the treatment of young adults diagnosed with mental illness and substance abuse.' *Music Therapy Perspectives 10*, 21–26.

Berridge, K.C. and Kringelbach, M.L. (2008) 'Affective neuroscience of pleasure: Reward in humans and animals.' *Psychopharmacology 199*, 3, 457–480.

Berry, R. and Sellman, J.D. (2001) 'Childhood adversity in alcohol- and drug-dependent women presenting to out-patient treatment.' *Drug and Alcohol Review 20*, 4, 361–367.

Bitcon, C. (2000) *Alike and Different: The Clinical and Educational Uses of Orff-Schulwerk*. Gilsum, NH: Barcelona.

Bjerg, O. (2008) 'Drug addiction and capitalism: Too close to the body.' *Body & Society 14*, 2, 1–22.

Blake, A. (2007) 'Drugs and Popular Music in the Modern Age.' In P. Manning (ed.) *Drugs and Popular Culture*, 103–116. Cullompton: Willan.

Blätter, A. (1990) *Kulturelle Ausprägungen und die Funktion des Drogengebrauchs [Cultural Profiles and Function of Drug Use]*. Hamburg: Wayasbah Verlag.

Blood, A.J. and Zatorre, R.J. (2001) 'Intensely pleasurable responses to music correlate with activity in brain regions implicated in reward and emotion.' *Proceedings of the National Academy of Sciences of the United States of America 98*, 20, 11818–11823.

Boecker, H., Sprenger, T., Spilker, M.E., Henriksen, G. *et al.* (2008) 'The runner's high: Opioidergic mechanisms in the human brain.' *Cerebral Cortex 18*, 11, 2523–2531.

Boening, J.A. (2001) 'Neurobiology of an addiction memory.' *Journal of Neural Transmission 108*, 6, 755–765.

Bondolfi, G., Jermann, F., Ferrero, F., Zullino, D. and Osiek, C.H. (2008) 'Prevalence of pathological gambling in Switzerland after the opening of casinos and the introduction of new preventive legislation.' *Acta Psychiatrica Scandinavica 117*, 3, 236–239.

Bonny, H. (1980) *GIM Therapy – Past, Present and Future Implications.* Salina: The Bonny Foundation.

Bonny, H. (2002) *Music and Consciousness: The Evolution of Guided Imagery and Music* (edited by Lisa Summer). Gilsum, NH: Barcelona.

Borczon, R.M. (1997) *Music Therapy: Group Vignettes.* Gilsum, NH: Barcelona.

Boyd, J. (1992) *Musicians in Tune – Seventy-Five Contemporary Musicians Discuss the Creative Process.* New York: Fireside, a Simon & Schuster imprimateur.

Brook, D.W. (2001) 'Introduction to the special issue on group therapy and substance abuse.' *International Journal of Group Psychotherapy 51*, 1, 5–11.

Brook, D.W. (2003) 'Exploring group therapies.' [Electronic Version]. *Psychiatric Times XX*, 2, 1–8.

Brown, P.J., Read, J.P. and Kahler, C.W. (2003) 'Comorbid Posttraumatic Stress Disorder and Substance Use Disorders: Treatment Outcomes and the Role of Coping.' In P. Ouimette and P.J. Brown (eds) *Trauma and Substance Abuse*, 171–188. Washington, DC: American Psychological Association.

Bruscia, K.E. (1987) *Improvisational Models of Music Therapy.* Springfield, IL: Charles C. Thomas.

Bruscia, K.E. (1996) 'Authenticity Issues in Qualitative Research'. In M. Langenberg, K. Aigen and J. Frommer (eds) *Qualitative Music Therapy Research: Beginning Dialogues*, 81–107. Gilsum, NH: Barcelona.

Bruscia, K.E. (1998) 'An Introduction to Music Psychotherapy.' In K.E. Bruscia (ed.) *The Dynamics of Music Psychotherapy*, 1–15. Gilsum, NH: Barcelona.

Campling, P. (1999) 'Chaotic Personalities: Maintaining the Therapeutic Alliance'. In P. Campling and R. Haigh (eds) *Therapeutic Communities: Past, Present and Future*, 127–139. London: Jessica Kingsley Publishers.

Carlezon, W.A. and Konradi, C. (2004) 'Understanding the neurobiological consequences of early exposure to psychotropic drugs: linking behavior with molecules.' *Neuropharmacology 47*, Suppl 1, 47–60.

Comeau, P. (2004) 'A Phenomenological Investigation of Being Effective as a Music Therapist.' In B. Abrams (ed.) *Qualitative Inquiries in Music Therapy: A Monograph Series (Vol. 1)*, 19–35. Gilsum, NH: Barcelona.

Cooper, M. (2003) *Existential Therapies.* London: Sage.

Cottler, L.B., Compton, W.M. and Mager, D. (1992) 'Posttraumatic stress disorder among substance users from the general population.' *American Journal of Psychiatry 149*, 5, 664–670.

Crowther, J.H. (1983) 'Stress management training and relaxation imagery in the treatment of essential hypertension.' *Journal of Behavioural Medicine 6*, 2, 169–187.

Dansky, B.S., Byrne, C.A. and Brady, K.T. (1999) 'Intimate violence and post-traumatic stress disorder among individuals with cocaine dependence.' *American Journal of Drug and Alcohol Abuse 25*, 2, 257–268.

De Jong, C.A.J. (2006) *Chronisch Verslaafd: De patiënt, de therapeut en de ziekte [Chronic Addiction: The patient, the therapist and the Disorder].* Inaugural lecture, Radboud Universiteit. Nijmegen: NISPA.

De Jong, C.A.J., van den Brink W., Harteveld, F.M. and van der Wielen, E.G.M. (1993) 'Personality disorders in alcoholic and drug addicts.' *Comprehensive Psychiatry 34*, 87–94.

De Leon, G. (1994). *Therapeutic Community: Advances in Research and Application.* National Institute on Drug Abuse, Research Monograph Series. Retrieved 25 January 2010 from www.drugabuse.gov/pdf/monographs/144.pdf.

De Leon, G. (1997) *Community as Method: Therapeutic Communities for Special Populations and Special Settings.* Westport, CT: Praeger.

De Leon, G. (2000) *The Therapeutic Community: Theory, Model, and Method.* New York: Springer.

DeNora, T. (2000) *Music in Everyday Life.* Cambridge: Cambridge University Press.

DeNure, B. (2006) 'Effective strategies for treating those with the illness of pathological gambling.' *Journal of Groups in Addiction and Recovery 27*, 1, 3–4.

Dijkstra, I.T.F. and De Jong, C.A.J. (2003) 'Theorie en praktijk van de klinische psychotherapie. Een therapeutische gemeenschap voor patiënten met afhankelijkheid van psychoactieve stoffen: Interpersoonlijk gedrag in actie ['Theory and Practice of Clinical Psychotherapy: A Therapeutic Community for Patients with Dependency on Psychoactive Substances; Interpersonal Behaviour in Action']. In C. Janzing, A. van den Berg and F. Kruisdijk (eds) *Handboek voor Milieutherapie deel* [Handbook of Social Environment Therapy] *2*, 135–155. Assen: Van Gorcum and Comp.

Dijkstra, I.T.F. and Hakvoort, L.G. (2004) 'How to deal music? Enhancing coping strategies in music therapy with clients suffering from addiction problems. *Music Therapy Today V* (5). Retrieved 25 January 25 2010 from www.musictherapytoday.com.

Dijkstra, I.T.F. and Hakvoort, L.G. (2006) 'Verslaving' ['Addiction']. In H. Smeijsters (ed.) *Handboek muziektherapie [Music Therapy Reference Book]*, 254–275. Baarn: Bohn Stafleu van Lochum.

Doak, B.A. (2003) 'Relationships between adolescent psychiatric diagnoses, music preferences and drug preferences.' *Music Therapy Perspectives 21, 2,* 69–76.

Dougherty, K. (1984) 'Music therapy in the treatment of the alcoholic client.' *Music Therapy 4,* 1, 47–54.

DuPont, R.L. (2000) *The Selfish Brain: Learning from Addiction.* Center City, MN: Hazelden.

Dutch Health Care Council (2002) *'Medicamenteuze interventies bij drugverslaving' ['Medicinal interventions with drug addiction']*. Retrieved 25 January 2010 from www.gezondheidsraad.nl/nl/adviezen/medicamenteuze-interventies-bij-drugverslaving.

Eadington, W. (1997) 'Understanding Gambling.' In W. Eadington and J. Cornelius (eds) *Gambling: Public Policies and the Social Sciences,* 3–9. Reno, NV: Institute for the Study of Gambling and Commercial Gaming, College of Business Administration, University of Nevada.

Eagle, C.T. (1972) 'Music and LSD: An empirical study.' *Journal of Music Therapy 9,* Spring, 23–36.

Eichel, G.R. and Troiden, R.R. (1978) 'The domestication of drug effects: The case of marihuana.' *Journal of Psychedelic Drugs 10, 2,* 133–136.

Eisen, S.A. (1998) 'Familial influences on gambling behaviour: An analysis of 3359 twin pairs.' *Addiction 93,* 9, 1375–1384.

Elliott, R., Newman, J.L., Longe, O.A. and Deakin, J.F. (2003) 'Differential response patterns in the striatum and orbitofrontal cortex to financial reward in humans: A parametric functional magnetic resonance imaging study.' *Journal of Neuroscience 23,* 1, 303–307.

Emrich, H.M. (1990) *Psychiatrische Anthropologie – Therapeutische Bedeutung von Phantasiesystemen [Psychiatric Anthropology – Therapeutic Impact of Fantasy Systems]*. München: Pfeiffer.

Engel, G.L. (1980) 'The clinical applications of the biopsychosocial model.' *American Journal of Psychiatry 137,* 5, 535–544.

Erk, S., Spitzer, M., Wunderlich, A.P., Galley, L. and Walter, H. (2002) 'Cultural objects modulate reward circuitry.' *Neuroreport 13,* 18, 2499–2503.

Erkkilä, J. (1997a) 'Musical improvisation and drawings as tools in the music therapy of children.' *Nordic Journal of Music Therapy 6,* 2, 112–120.

Erkkilä, J. (1997b) *Musiikin merkitystasot musiikkiterapian teorian ja kliinisen käytännön näkökulmista [Levels of Musical Meaning from Theoretical and Clinical Perspectives on Music Therapy]*. Unpublished Doctoral Dissertation (PhD), Department of Music, University of Jyväskylä.

Erkkilä, J. (2003). 'Music therapy methods in the treatment of gambling addiction' [Electronic Version]. *Music Therapy Today IV,* 3. Retrieved 12 October 2009 from www.musictherapyworld.de/modules/mmmagazine/issues/20030613105603/20030613111033/Erkkila_MTT.pdf.

Erkkilä, J. and Eerola, T. (2001) *Hallitsetko sinä pelejä vai pelit sinua? Tutkimus ongelmapelaajien monimenetelmäisestä kuntoutusprojektista [Can You Control Your Gambling? Research Report on Multimethodic Treatment Programme for People with Gambling Addiction]*. Jyväskylä: Suomen Musiikkiterapiayhdistys r. y.

Esch, T. and Stefano, G.B. (2004) 'The neurobiology of pleasure, reward processes, addiction and their health implications.' *Neuroendocrinology Letters 25,* 4, 235–251.

Fachner, J. (2002) 'The Space between the Notes - Research on Cannabis and Music Perception.' In K. Kärki, R. Leydon and H. Terho (eds) *Looking Back, Looking Ahead – Popular Music Studies 20 Years Later,* 308–319. Turku, Finland: IASPM-Norden.

Fachner, J. (2004a) 'CLEAN UP! "Heimatschutz", Anti-Drogenpolitik und legislative Auswirkungen auf die Rave-Kultur nach dem 11 September 2001' ['CLEAN UP!' "Homeland Security", Anti-Drug Policy and Legislative Action on Rave Culture after 9/11']. In D. Helms and T. Phleps (eds) *9/11 – The World's All Out of Tune - Populäre Musik nach dem 11 September 2001 [Popular Music after 9/11]*, 81–98. Bielefeld: Transkript Verlag.

Fachner, J. (2004b) 'Jazz Improvisation and a Social Pharmacology of Music.' In J. Fachner and D. Aldridge (eds) *Music Therapy in the 21st Century: A Contemporary Force for Change – E-Book of Articles,* 488–513. Witten: MusicTherapyWorld.net.

Fachner, J. (2006a) 'Music and Altered States of Consciousness – An Overview.' In D. Aldridge and J. Fachner (eds) *Music and Altered States – Consciousness, Transcendence, Therapy and Addictions.* 15–37. London: Jessica Kingsley Publishers.

Fachner, J. (2006b) 'Music and Drug Induced Altered States of Consciousness.' In D. Aldridge and J. Fachner (eds) *Music and Altered States – Consciousness, Transcendence, Therapy and Addictions,* 82–96. London: Jessica Kingsley Publishers.

Fachner, J. (2007). 'Takin' it to the Streets… Psychotherapie, Drogen und Psychedelic rock' [Electronic Version]. *Samples 6.* Retrieved 30 October 2007 from www.aspm-samples.de.

Fals-Stewart, W., O'Farrel, T.J. and Birchler, G.R. (2003) 'Family Therapy Techniques.' In F. Rotgers, J. Morgenstern and S.T. Walters (eds) *Treating Substance Abuse: Theory and Technique*, 2nd edition, 140–165. New York: Guilford Press.

Ferrara, A. (1993) *Modernity and Authenticity: A Study of the Social and Ethical Thought of Jean-Jacques Rousseau.* New York: State University of New York Press.

Ficken, T. (1976) 'The use of songwriting in a psychiatric setting.' *Journal of Music Therapy 14*, 4, 163–172.

Flores, P.J. (2001) 'Addiction as an attachment disorder: Implications for group therapy.' *International Journal of Group Psychotherapy 51*, 1, 63–82.

Folkman, S. and Lazarus, R.S. (1984) *Stress, Appraisal, and Coping.* New York: Springer

Forinash, M. (1990) 'A phenomenology of music therapy with the terminally ill' [Doctoral dissertation, New York University]. *Dissertation Abstracts International 51(09)*, 2915A.

Forinash, M. (1993) 'An exploration into qualitative research in music therapy.' *The Arts in Psychotherapy 20*, 1, 69–73.

Forinash, M. and Gonzales, D. (1989) 'A phenomenological perspective of music therapy.' *Music Therapy 8*, 1, 35–46.

Forinash, M. and Grocke, D. (2005) 'Phenomenological Inquiry.' In B.L. Wheeler (ed.) *Music Therapy Research*, 2nd edition, 321–334. Gilsum, NH: Barcelona.

Forsyth, A.J.M., Barnard, M. and McKeganey, N.P. (1997) 'Musical preference as an indicator of adolescent drug use.' *Addiction 92*, 10, 1317–1325.

Franck-Schwebel, A. (2002) 'Developmental Trauma and Its Relation to Sound and Music.' In J.P. Sutton (ed.) *Music, Music Therapy and Trauma.* London: Jessica Kingsley Publishers.

Freed, B.S. (1987) 'Songwriting with the chemically dependent.' *Music Therapy Perspectives 4*, 13–18.

Freeman, W. (2000) 'A Neurobiological Role of Music in Social Bonding.' In N.L. Wallin, B. Merker and S. Brown (eds) *The Origins of Music.* 411–424. Cambridge, MA: MIT Press.

Frith, S. (1987) 'Towards an Aesthetic of Popular Music.' In R. Leppert and S. McClary (eds.) *Music and Society: The Politics of Composition, Performance and Reception*, 133–150. Cambridge: Cambridge University Press.

Frith, S. (1998) *Performing Rites.* Oxford: Oxford University Press.

Gahlinger, P.M. (2004) 'Club drugs: MDMA, gamma-hydroxybutyrate (GHB), rohypnol, and ketamine.' *American Family Physician 69*, 11, 2619–2626.

Gallagher, L.M. and Steele, A.L. (2002) 'Music therapy with offenders in a substance abuse/mental illness treatment program.' *Music Therapy Perspectives 20*, 2, 117–122.

Gallant, W., Holosko, M. and Siegel, S. (1997) 'The use of music in counselling addictive clients.' *Journal of Alcohol and Drug Education 42*, 2, 42–52.

Garrett, J., Landau-Stanton, J., Stanton, J., Stellato-Kabat, J. and Stellato-Kabat, D. (1997) 'ARISE: A method for engaging reluctant alcohol- and drug-dependent individuals in treatment.' *Journal of Substance Abuse Treatment 14*, 3, 235–248.

Gelpke, R. (1982) *Vom Rausch im Orient und Okzident [Being under the Influence in Orient and Occident].* Frankfurt: Klett-Cotta im Ullstein Taschenbuch Verlag.

Gerhard, H. (2001) 'Party-drugs: Sociocultural and individual background and risks.' *International Journal of Clinical Pharmacology and Therapeutics 39*, 8, 362–366.

Ghetti, C.M. (2004) 'Incorporating music therapy into the harm reduction approach to managing substance use problems.' *Music Therapy Perspectives 22*, 2, 84–90.

Glicksohn, J. (1993) 'Altered sensory environments, altered states of consciousness and altered-state cognition.' *The Journal of Mind and Behaviour 14*, 1, 1–12.

Globus, G.G., Cohen, H.B., Kramer, J.C., Elliot, H.W. and Sharp, R. (1978) 'Effects of marihuana induced altered state of consciousness on auditory perception.' *Journal of Psychedelic Drugs 10*, 1, 71–76.

Goldberg, F. (1992) 'Images and emotion: The role of emotions in guided imagery and music.' *Journal of the Association of Music and Imagery 1*, 5–18.

Goldstein, A. (1980) 'Thrills in response to music and other stimuli.' *Physiological Psychology 8*, 1, 126–129.

Golomb, J. (1995) *In Search of Authenticity: From Kierkegaard to Camus.* London: Routledge.

Gouzoulis-Mayfrank, E., Hermle, L., Thelen, B. and Sass, H. (1998) 'History, rationale and potential of human experimental hallucinogenic drug research in psychiatry.' *Pharmacopsychiatry 31*, Suppl 2, 63–68.

Gowen, D. and Speyerer, J.B. (1995) 'Compulsive gambling and the criminal offender: A treatment and supervision approach.' *Federal Probation 59*, 3, 36–39.

Grant, J.E., Williams, K.A. and Kim, S.W. (2006) 'Update on pathological gambling.' *Current Psychiatry Reports 8*, 1, 53–58.

Gray, M.T. (2004) 'Philosophical inquiry in nursing: An argument for radical empiricism as a philosophical framework for the phenomenology of addiction.' *Qualitative Health Research 14*, 8, 1151–1164.

Grinberg, L. and Grinberg, R. (1984) *Psychoanalytic Perspectives on Migration and Exile.* New Haven and London: Yale University Press.

Grocke, D. (1999) *A Phenomenological Study of Pivotal Moments in Guided Imagery and Music (GIM) Therapy.* Unpublished Doctoral Dissertation, University of Melbourne, Australia.

Grocke, D. and Wigram, T. (2007) *Receptive Methods in Music Therapy: Techniques and Applications for Music Therapy Clinicians, Educators and Students.* London: Jessica Kingsley Publishers.

Hairo-Lax, U. (2005) *Musiikkiterapiaprosessin merkittävät tekijät ja merkittävät hetket päihteettömän elämäntavan tukijoina [Significant Moments and Significant Factors of Music Therapy in the Process of Supporting an Intoxicant-Free way of Life].* Sibelius-Akatemia. Musiikkikasvatuksen osasto. Studia Musica 27. Väitöskirja.

Hakvoort, L.G. (2002) 'Observation and Treatment Criteria in Music Therapy for Forensic Patients.' In J. Fachner and D. Aldridge (2004) *Dialogue and Debate: Proceedings of the 10th World Congress on Music Therapy*, 723–744. Witten: MusicTherapyWorld.net.

Hakvoort, L.G. (2008) 'Rapmuziektherapie: Een muzikale methodiek' ['Rap music therapy: A musical methodology']. *Tijdschrift voor Vaktherapie 4*, 4, 15–21.

Havoort, L. and Dijkstra, I. (2007) 'Music therapy and addiction – can research support its effect?' *Music Therapy Today, 3.* Retrieved 03 March 2010 from http://musictherapyworld.net

Hammer, S.E. (1996) 'The effect of guided imagery through music on state and trait anxiety.' *Journal of Music Therapy 33*, 1, 47–70.

Hedigan, J. (2005) 'Music therapy in a therapeutic community: Bringing the music to the players'. [Electronic Version] *Music Therapy Today VI*, 1 (February), .5–22. Retrieved 25 January 2010 from www.musictherapyworld.com

Hedigan, J.P. (2008) *The Experience of Group Music Therapy for Substance Dependent Adults Living in a Therapeutic Community.* Unpublished Masters Thesis, University of Melbourne, Australia.

Heidegger, M. (1962) *Being and Time* (J. Macquarrie and E. Robinson, Trans.). Oxford: Blackwell. (Original work published 1926.)

Hirschman, E.C. (1995) 'Professional, personal, and popular culture perspectives on addiction'. *American Behavioral Scientist 38*, 4, 537–552.

Hogan, B. (1999) 'The Experience of Music Therapy for Terminally Ill Patients.' In R.R. Pratt and D. Grocke (eds) *Music Medicine 3*, 242–252. Melbourne, Australia: Faculty of Music, University of Melbourne.

Horesh, T. (2006a) 'Dangerous Music – Working with the Destructive and Healing Powers of Popular Music in the Treatment of Substance Abusers.' In D. Aldridge and J. Fachner (Eds.) *Music and Altered States – Consciousness, Transcendence, Therapy and Addictions,* 125–139. London: Jessica Kingsley Publishers.

Horesh, T. (2006b) "Music is my whole life" – The many meanings of music in addicts' lives' [Electronic Version]. *Music Therapy Today VII*, 2. Retrieved 25 January 2010 from www.musictherapyworld.net.

Horesh, T. (2006c) "Music is my whole life" – the challenges of music therapy in a therapeutic community'. [in Hebrew]. *Therapy through the Arts 4*, 1, 31–35.

Horesh.T. (2007a) *The Many Meanings of Music in the Lives of Drug Addicts Undergoing Treatment and Rehabilitation* [in Hebrew] Unpublished MA Thesis, Hebrew University, Israel. Retrieved 25 January 2010 from www.antidrugs.org.il/template/default.asp?maincat=12&catId=41&pageId=1153&parentId=227.

Horesh, T. (2007b). 'Music therapy, regression and symbolic distance in substance abusers and their preferred music' [Electronic Version]. *Music Therapy Today VIII*, 3. Retrieved 9 January 2008 from www.musictherapyworld. net/modules/mmmagazine/issues/20080108093144/20080108095933/MTT8_3_Horesh.pdf.

Horn, B.P. (1997) 'Is there a cure for America's gambling addiction?' *USA Today Magazine 125*, 2624, 34–37.

Howard, M.M.A.A. (1997) 'The effects of music and poetry therapy on the treatment of women and adolescents with chemical addictions.' *Journal of Poetry Therapy 11*, 2, 81–102.

Humphreys, K., Wing, S., McCarty, D., Chappel, J. *et al.* (2004) 'Self-help organizations for alcohol and drug problems: Toward evidence-based practice and policy.' *Journal of Substance Abuse Treatment 26*, 151–158.

Jaakkola, T. (2006) *Viihteestä riippuvuudeksi – rahapeliongelmien luonne.* [Entertainment Dependency: The Gambling Nature of the Problem] Retrieved 15 December 2006 from www.stat.fi/artikkelit/2006/art_2006-12-13_002.html.

Jackson, D. (1965) 'The study of the family.' *Family Process 4*, 1–20.

James, M.R. (1988a) 'Music therapy and alcoholism: I. An overview of the addiction.' *Music Therapy Perspectives 5*, 60–64.

James, M.R. (1988b) 'Music therapy and alcoholism: II. Treatment services.' *Music Therapy Perspectives 5*, 65–68.

Johnson, B. (1999) 'Three perspectives on addiction.' *Journal of the American Psychoanalytic Association 47*, 3, 791–815.

Jones, J.D. (1998) *A Comparison of Songwriting and Lyric Analysis to Evoke Emotional Change in a Single Session with Chemically Dependent Clients.* Unpublished Master's Thesis, Florida State University, Tallahassee.

Jones, J.D. (2005) 'A comparison of songwriting and lyric analysis techniques to evoke emotional change in a single session with people who are chemically dependent.' *Journal of Music Therapy 42*, 2, 94–110.

Jonnes, J. (1999) *Hep-Cats, Narcs and Pipe Dreams*. Baltimore: Johns Hopkins University Press.

Julien, R.M., Advokat, C.D. and Comaty, J.E. (2008) *A Primer of Drug Action: A Comprehensive Guide to the Actions, Uses, and Side Effects of Psychoactive Drugs*. New York: Worth Publishers.

Jungaberle, H., Ullrich-Kleinmanns, J., Weinhold, J. and Verres, R. (2008) 'Muster und Verlauf des Konsums psychoaktiver Substanzen im Jugendalter – Die Bedeutung von Kohärenzsinn und Risikowahrnehmung ['Patterns and progress of psychoactive drug consumption in adolescence – The impact of a sense of coherence and risk perception']. *Suchttherapie 9*, 1, 12–21.

Juslin, P.N. and Västfjäll, D. (2008) 'Emotional responses to music: The need to consider underlying mechanisms.' *Behavioral and Brain Sciences 31*, 5, 559–575.

Kabbaj, M., Evans, S., Watson, S.J. and Akil, H. (2004) 'The search for the neurobiological basis of vulnerability to drug abuse: Using microarrays to investigate the role of stress and individual differences.' *Neuropharmacology 47 Suppl 1*, 111–122.

Kaikkonen, M. (2008) 'Figurenotes allows all to make music.' *Room 217 Newsletter*, Issue 8, October. Retrieved 25 January 2010 from www.room217.ca/newsletter/index.php?article=105.

Kärki, K., Leydon, R. and Terho, H. (eds) (2002) *Looking Back, Looking Ahead – Popular Music Studies 20 Years Later*. Turku: IASPM Norden.

Kaufman, E. (1994) *Psychotherapy of Addicted Persons*. New York and London: Guilford Press.

Keen, A.W. (2004) 'Using music as a therapy to motivate troubled adolescents.' *Social Work Health Care 39*, 3–4, 361–373.

Kernberg, O.F. (1984) *Severe Personality Disorders: Psychotherapeutic Strategies*. New Haven and London: Yale University Press.

Kerouac, J. (1962) *Big Sur*. London: Penguin.

Khantzian, E.J. (1985) 'The self-medication hypothesis of addictive disorders: Focus on heroin and cocaine dependence.' *American Journal of Psychiatry 142*, 11, 1259–1264.

Khantzian, E.J., Halliday, K.S., and McAuliffe, W.E. (1990) *Addiction and the Vulnerable Self: Modified Dynamic Group Therapy for Substance Abusers*. New York: Guilford Press.

Kilpatrick, D.G., Acierno, R., Resnick, H.S., Saunders, B.E. and Best, C.L. (1997) 'A 2-year longitudinal analysis of the relationships between violent assault and substance use in women.' *Journal of Consulting and Clinical Psychology 65*, 5, 834–847.

Knutson, B., Westdorp, A., Kaiser, E. and Hommer, D. (2000) 'FMRI visualization of brain activity during a monetary incentive delay task.' *Neuroimage 12*, 1, 20–27.

Kohlmetz, C., Kopiez, R. and Altenmüller, E. (2003) 'Stability of motor programs during a state of meditation: Electrocortical activity in a pianist playing "Vexations" by Erik Satie continuously for 28 hours.' *Psychology of Music 31*, 2, 173–186.

Kohut, H. and Levarie, S. (1990) 'On the Enjoyment of Listening to Music.' In S. Feder, R.L. Karmel and G.H. Pollock (eds) *Psychoanalytic Explorations in Music*, 21–38. Madison, CT: International Universities Press. (Original work published in *Psychoanalytic Quarterly 19*, 64–87, 1950.)

Kooyman, M. (1993) *The Therapeutic Community for Addicts: Intimacy, Parent Involvement and Treatment Success*. Amsterdam: Swets and Zeitlinger.

Kopiez, R., Bangert, M., Goebl, W. and Altenmüller, E. (2003) 'Tempo and loudness analysis of a continuous 28-hour performance of Erik Satie's composition "Vexations".' *Journal of New Music Research 32*, 3, 243–258.

Kramer, D. (1997) '"Ask the gambling question," FPs told as "secret" addiction becomes more common.' *Canadian Medical Association Journal 157*, 1, 61–63.

Kvale, S. (1996) *Interviews: An Introduction to Qualitative Research Interviewing*. Thousand Oaks, CA: Sage.

Laing, R.D. (1960) *The Divided Self: An Existential Study in Sanity and Madness*. London: Tavistock.

Laing, R.D. (1961) *Self and Others*. London: Tavistock.

Laing, R.D. (1967) *The Politics of Experience*. New York: Pantheon Books.

Lamberti, J. (1999) 'Therapeutic Communities.' In *Heroin Crisis*, 163–168. Melbourne, Australia: Bookman Press.

Lehikoinen, P. (1997) 'The Physioacoustic Method.' In T. Wigram and C. Dileo (eds) *Music, Vibration and Health*, 209–215. Cherry Hill, NJ: Jeffrey Books.

Lehikoinen, P., and Kanstren, J. (1996) *Corporate Health Care Experiment at the Sibelius Academy*. Helsinki, Finland: Sibelius Academy.

Lehtonen, K. (2002) 'Some ideas about music therapy for the elderly.' *Voices: A World Forum for Music Therapy*. Retrieved 22 July 2004 from www.voices.no/mainissues/Voices2(1)lehtonen.html.

Leshner, A. (1997) 'Drug abuse and addiction treatment research: The next generation.' *Archives of General Psychiatry 54*, 8, 691–694.

Levitin, D. (2008) *This is Your Brain on Music*. London: Atlantic Books.

Leweke, F.M., Giuffrida, A., Wurster, U., Emrich, H.M. and Piomelli, D. (1999) 'Elevated endogenous cannabinoids in schizophrenia.' *Neuroreport 10*, 8, 1665–1669.

Lofwall, M.R., Griffiths, R.R. and Mintzer, M.Z. (2006) 'Cognitive and subjective acute dose effects of intramuscular ketamine in healthy adults.' *Experimental and Clinical Psychopharmacology 14*, 4, 439–449.

Lopes, P. (2005) 'Signifying deviance and transgression: Jazz in the popular imagination.' *American Behavioral Scientist 48*, 11, 1468–1481.

Lozanov, G. (1978) *Suggestology and Outlines of Suggestopedy.* New York: Gordon and Breach.

Lull, J. (1987) 'Listeners' Communicative Uses of Popular Music.' In J. Lull (ed.) *Popular Music and Communication, 140–174.* Beverly Hills, CA: Sage Publishers.

Lyttle, T. and Montagne, M. (1992) 'Drugs, music, and ideology: A social pharmacological interpretation of the Acid House Movement.' *The International Journal of the Addictions 27*, 10, 1159–1177.

Machleidt, W., Gutjahr, L. and Mugge, A. (1989) 'Grundegefühle: Phänomenologie, Psychodynamik, EEG-Sperkralanalytik' ['Basic emotions: Phenomenology, psychodynamics, EEG spectral analysis']. *Monographien der Gesamtgebiete der Psychiatrie – Psychiatry Serials 57*, 1–251.

Mahler, S.V., Smith, K.S. and Berridge, K.C. (2007) 'Endocannabinoid hedonic hotspot for sensory pleasure: Anandamide in nucleus accumbens shell enhances "liking" of a sweet reward.' *Neuropsychopharmacology 32*, 11, 2267–2278.

Main, M. and Hesse, E. (1990) 'Parents' Unresolved Traumatic Experiences are Related to Infant Disorganized Attachment Status: Is Frightened and/or Frightening Parental Behavior the Linking Mechanism?' In M. Greenberg, D. Cicchetti and E. Cummings (eds) *Attachment in the Preschool Years: Theory, Research and Intervention*, 161–182. Chicago: University of Chicago Press.

Manning, P. (2007) *Drugs and Popular Culture – Drugs, Media and Identity in Contemporary Society.* Cullompton: Willan Publishing.

Mark, A. (1986) 'Adolescents discuss themselves and drugs through music.' *Journal of Substance Abuse Treatment 3*, 4, 243–249.

Mark, A. (1988) 'Metaphoric lyrics as a bridge to the adolescent's world.' *Adolescence 23*, 90, 313–323.

Markert, J. (2001) 'Sing a song of drug use-abuse: Four decades of drug lyrics in popular music – From the sixties through the nineties.' *Sociological Inquiry 71*, 2, 194–220.

Marlatt, A. and Donovan, D. (eds). (2005) *Relapse Prevention: Maintenance Strategies in the Treatment of Addictive Behaviors*, 2nd Edition. New York: The Guilford Press.

Marlatt, A. and Gordon, J. (eds) (1985) *Relapse Prevention: Maintenance Strategies in the Treatment of Addictive Behaviors.* New York: The Guilford Press.

Masters, R.E.L. and Houston, J. (1968) *Psychedelic Art.* London: Weidenfeld & Nicolson.

Mastnak, W. (1993) 'Musik-Hypnotherapie bei psychiatrischen Patienten' ['Music hypnotherapy with psychiatric patients']. *Musiktherapeutische Umschau XIV*, 4, 306–316.

Mays, K.L., Clark, D.L. and Gordon, A.J. (2008) 'Treating addiction with tunes: A systematic review of music therapy for the treatment of patients with addictions.' *Substance Abuse 29*, 4, 51–59.

McClung, C.A., Ulery, P.G., Perrotti, L.I., Zachariou, V., Berton, O. and Nestler, E.J. (2004) 'DeltaFosB: A molecular switch for long-term adaptation in the brain.' *Brain Research 132*, 2, 146–154.

McKenna, T.K. (1992) *Food of the Gods: The Search for the Original Tree of Knowledge. A Radical History of Plants, Drugs, and Human Evolution.* New York: Bantam Books.

McKenna, W.R. (1982) *Husserl's 'Introductions to Phenomenology': Interpretation and Critique.* The Hague, Netherlands: Martinus Nijhoff.

McLellan, A.T., Luborsky, L., Woody, G.E. and O'Brien, C.P. (1980) 'An improved diagnostic instrument for substance abuse patients: The Addiction Severity Index.' *Journal of Nervous & Mental Diseases 168*, 1, 26–33.

Mellgren, A. (1979) 'Hypnotherapy and art (vocalists and musicians).' *The Journal of the American Society of Psychosomatic Dentistry and Medicine 26*, 4, 152–155.

Mello, D.O., Pechansky, F., Inciardi, J.A. and Surratt, H.L. (1997) 'Participant observation of a therapeutic community model for offenders in drug treatment.' *Journal of Drug Issues 27*, 2, 299–314.

Meszaros, I., Szabo, C. and Csako, R.I. (2002) 'Hypnotic susceptibility and alterations in subjective experiences.' *Acta Biologica Hungarica 53*, 4, 499–514.

Metzner, R. (1992) 'Molekulare Mystik: Die Rolle psychoaktiver Substanzen bei der Transformation des Bewußtseins' ['Molecular Mystics: The Role of Psychoactive Substances during Transformation of Consciousness'] In C. Rätsch (Ed.) *Das Tor zu den inneren Räumen* [The Doors to the Inner Spaces] 63–78. Südergellsen: Verlag Bruno Martin.

Miller, G. (2005) *Learning the Language of Addiction Counselling.* Hoboken, NJ: John Wiley and Sons.

Miranda, R., Meyerson, L.A., Long, P.J., Marx, B.P. and Simpson, S.M. (2002) 'Sexual assault and alcohol use: Exploring the self-medication hypothesis.' *Violence and Victims 17*, 2, 205–217.

Moore, K. (2005) '"Sort Drugs Make Mates": The Use and Meaning of Mobiles in Dance Music Club Culture.' In B. Brown and K. O'Hara (eds) *Consuming Music Together: Social and Collaborative Aspects of Music Consumption Technologies*, 211–239. Netherlands: Springer.

Moran, E. (1970) 'Varieties of pathological gambling.' *British Journal of Psychiatry 116*, 535, 593–597.

Murphy, M. (1983) 'Music therapy: A self-help group experience for substance abuse patients.' *Music Therapy 3*, 1, 52–62.

Murphy, S.L. and Khantzian, E.J. (1995) 'Addiction as a "Self-Medication" Disorder: Application of Ego Psychology to the Treatment of Substance Abuse.' In A.M. Washton (ed.) *Psychotherapy and Substance Abuse: A Practitioner's Handbook*, 161–175. New York: Guilford Press.

Nathanson, D.L. (1989) 'Denial, Projection and the Empathic Wall.' In E.L. Edelstein, D.L. Nathanson and A.M. Stone (eds) *Denial: A Clarification of Concepts and Research*, 37–55. New York: Plenum Press.

Nencini, P. (2002) 'The shaman and the rave party: Social pharmacology of ecstasy.' *Substance Use & Misuse 37*, 8–10, 923–939.

Nestler, E.J. (2004) 'Molecular mechanisms of drug addiction.' *Neuropharmacology 47 Suppl 1*, 24–32.

NIDA (2005) 'What is a Therapeutic Community?' Retrieved 15 May 2005 *www.drugabuse.gov/ResearchReports/ Therapeutic/Therapeutic2.html*.

Nolan, P. (2005) 'Verbal processing within the music therapy relationship.' *Music Therapy Perspectives 23*, 1, 18–28.

Nolte, N. (1991) 'Der Unmutston' ['Sounds of Unpleasure']. In N. Nolte (ed.) *Walther von der Vogelweide: Höfische Idealität und Konkrete Erfahrung [Walther von der Vogelweide: Courtly Ideal and Concrete Experience]*, 19–65. Stuttgart: Hirzel.

Nordoff, P. and Robbins, C. (2007) *Creative Music Therapy: A Guide to Fostering Clinical Musicianship*, revised 2nd edition (with 4 CDs). Gilsum, NH: Barcelona.

O'Brien, C.P. (2008) 'Evidence-based treatments of addiction.' *Philosophical Transactions of the Royal Society B: Biological Sciences 363*, 1507, 3277–3286.

Olds, J. and Milner, P. (1954) 'Positive reinforcement produced by electrical stimulation of the septal area and other regions of the rat brain.' *Journal of Comparative and Physiological Psychology 47*, 6, 419–428.

Ortiz, J.M. (1997) *The Tao of Music*. York Beacg, ME: Samuel Weiser.

Panksepp, J. and Bernatzky, G. (2002) 'Emotional sounds and the brain: The neuro-affective foundations of musical appreciation.' *Behavioural Processes 60*, 2, 133–155.

Parker, H., Williams, L. and Aldridge, J. (2002) 'The normalization of "sensible" recreational drug use: Further evidence from the North West England Longitudinal Study.' *Sociology 36*, 4, 941–964.

Pavalko, R.M. (1999) 'Problem gambling.' *National Forum 79*, 4, 28–33.

Pelletier, C.L. (2004) 'The effect of music on decreasing arousal due to stress: A meta-analysis.' *Journal of Music Therapy XLI*, 3, 192–214.

Peters, R.K., Benson, H. and Peters, J.M. (1977) 'Daily relaxation response breaks in a working population: II. Effects on blood pressure.' *American Journal of Public Health 67*, 10, 954–959.

Philips, H. (2003). 'The pleasure seekers.' *New Scientist, 2416*, 36–43.

Pinson, P. (1991) 'Creating sacred space in prisons.' *Mentor 3*,1, 8–9.

Plutchik, R. (1984) 'Emotions and imagery.' *Journal of Mental Imagery 8*, 4, 105–111.

Polkinghorne, D.E. (1989) 'Phenomenological Research Methods.' In R.S. Valle and S. Halling (eds) *Existential-Phenomenological Perspectives in Psychology*, 41–60. New York: Plenum Press.

Potenza, M.N. (2005) 'Advancing treatment strategies for pathological gambling.' *Journal of Gambling Studies 21*, 1, 91–100.

Primack, B.A., Dalton, M.A., Carroll, M.V., Agarwal, A.A. and Fine, M.J. (2008) 'Content analysis of tobacco, alcohol, and other drugs in popular music.' *Archives of Pediatric and Adolescence Medicine 162*, 2, 169–175.

Punkanen, M. (2002) *'Matkalla mieleen ja tunteisiin': Fysioakustinen menetelmä ja musiikkiterapia huumekuntoutuksessa ['On a Journey to Mind and Emotions': Physioacoustic Method amnd Music Therapy in Drug Rehabilitation].* Unpublished Thesis (Pro gradu-tutkielma), University of Jyväskylä, Department of Music.

Punkanen, M. (2006a) *Musiikkiterapia osana huumekuntoutusta: Hoitoon kiinnittämisestä kokemusmaailman integroimiseen [Music Therapy as a Part of Drug Rehabilitation: From Adhering to Treatment to Integrating the Levels of Experience].* Unpublished Thesis (Lisensiaatintutkimus), University of Jyväskylä, Department of Music.

Punkanen, M. (2006b) 'On a Journey to Somatic Memory: Theoretical and Clinical Approaches for the Treatment of Traumatic Memories in Music Therapy-Based Drug Rehabilitation.' In D. Aldridge and J. Fachner (eds) *Music and Altered States: Consiousness, Transcendence, Therapy and Addictions*, 140–154. London: Jessica Kingsley Publishers.

Punkanen, M. (2007). 'Music therapy as a part of drug rehabilitation' [Electronic Version]. *Music Therapy Today VIII*, 3. Retrieved 9 January 2008 from www.musictherapyworld.net/modules/mmmagazine/issues/200801 08093144/20080108100021/MTT8_3_Punkanen.pdf.

Racette, K. (2004) 'A Phenomenological Analysis of the Experience of Listening to Music when Upset.' In B. Abrams (ed.) *Qualitative Inquiries in Music Therapy: A Monograph Series (Vol. 1)*, 1–17. Gilsum, NH: Barcelona.

Rainforth, M.V., Schneider, R.H., Nidich, S.I., Gaylord-King, C., Salerno, J.W. and Anderson, J.W. (2007) 'Stress reduction programs in patients with elevated blood pressure: A systematic review and meta-analysis.' *Current Hypertension Reports* 9, 6, 520–528.

Ratey, J.J. and Johnson, C. (1997) *Shadow Syndromes*. New York: Pantheon Books.

Rätsch, C. (Ed.) (1992) *Das Tor zu inneren Räumen [The Door to the Inner Spaces]*. Südergellsen: Verlag Bruno Martin.

Rätsch, C. (1995) *Heilkräuter der Antike in Ägypten, Griechenland und Rom - Mytologie und Anwendung [Healing Herbs of Ancient Egypt, Greece and Rome – Mythology and Usage]*. Munich: Eugen Diederichs Verlag.

Rätsch, C. (2005) *The Encyclopedia of Psychoactive Plants: Ethnopharmacology and Its Applications*. Rochester, VT: Park Street Press.

Reed, E.C. (1994) 'Basic Principles of Drug Use.' In M.J. Landry (ed.) *Understanding Drugs of Abuse: The Processes of Addiction, Treatment and Recovery*, 7–28. Washington, DC: American Psychiatric Press, Inc.

Reich, W. and Wolfe, T.P. (1945) *The Sexual Revolution: Toward a Self-Governing Character Structure*. New York: Orgone Institute Press.

Reith, G. (1999). 'In search of lost time: Recall, projection and the phenomenology of addiction.' *Time & Society* 8, 1, 99–117.

Rill, B. (2006) 'Rave, communitas, and embodied idealism' [Electronic Version]. *Music Therapy Today VII*, 3, 648–661. Retrieved 2 October 2006 from www.musictherapyworld.net/modules/mmmagazine/issues/2006092 9134150/20060929134848/MTT7_3_Rill.pdf.

Rittner, S. (2006) 'Trance und Rituale in Psychotherapie und Forschung' ['Rituals in Psychotherapy and Research']. In H. Jungaberle, R. Verres and F. DuBois (eds) *Rituale Erneueren – Ritualdynamik und Grenzerfahrung aus Interdisziplinärer Perspektive [Rituals Renewed – Ritual Dynamics and Peak Experience from an Interdisciplinary Perspective]*, 165–191. Giessen: Psychosozial.

Roberts, D., Henriksen, L. and Christenson, P. (1999) 'Substance use in popular movies and music.' Retrieved 5 June 1999 from http://ncadi.samhsa.gov/govstudy/medicstudy.new.aspx#_Toc447073447.

Robin, R. (2005) 'Adults in recovery: A year with members of the choirhouse.' *Nordic Journal of Music Therapy 14*, 2, 107–119.

Romanowski, B. (2007) 'Benefits and limitations of music therapy with psychiatric patients in the penitentiary system' [Electronic Version]. *Music Therapy Today VIII*, 3. Retrieved 20 September 2009 from www.musictherapyworld.de/modules/mmmagazine/issues/20080108093144/20080108100853/MTT8_3_Romanowski.pdf.

Ross, S., Cidambi, I., Dermatis, H., Weinstein, J. *et al.* (2008) 'Music therapy: A novel motivational approach for dually diagnosed patients.' *Journal of Addictive Diseases 27*, 1, 41–53.

Rotgers, F. (2003) 'Cognitive-Behavioural Theories of Substance Abuse.' In F. Rotgers, J. Morgenstern, and S.T. Walters (eds.) *Treating Substance Abuse: Theory and Technique*, 2nd edition, 166–189. New York: Guilford Press.

Rotgers, F., Morgenstern, J. and Walters, S.T. (2003) *Treating Substance Abuse: Theory and Technique*. New York: The Guilford Press.

Ruiz, P., Strain, E.C., and Langrod, J.G. (2007) *The Substance Abuse Handbook*. Philadelphia, PA: Lippincott, Williams and Wilkins.

Ruud, E. (1997) 'Music and the quality of life.' *Nordic Journal of Music Therapy 6*, 2, 86–97.

Ryynänen, E. (2004) *'Mie haluun hoitaa itteni kuntoon' Hoitomallin kehittämisprojekti huumevieroituspotilaan kuntoutumisen käynnistäjänä ['I Want to Get Myself in Better Sahpe': Developoment Project for Drug Rehabilitation]*. Unpublished Thesis (Pro gradu-tutkielma), University of Jyväskylä, Department of Music.

Sanders, B. (2005) 'In the club: Ecstasy use and supply in a London nightclub.' *Sociology 39*, 2, 241–258.

Sartre, J.P. (2003) *Being and Nothingness* (H.E. Barnes, Trans.). London: Routledge. (Original work published 1943.)

Schore, A.N. (1994) *Affect Regulation and the Origin of the Self: The Neurobiology of Emotional Development*. Hillsdale: Erlbaum.

Schore, A.N. (2003) *Affect Regulation and the Repair of the Self*. New York and London: W.W. Norton & Company.

Schotsmans, M. (2007) 'Music therapy with youngsters addicted to drugs, alcohol or medication: From the Sirens to Orpheus' [Electronic Version]. *Music Therapy Today VIII*, 3. REtrieved 25 January 2010 from www.musictherapyworld.net/modules/mmmagazine/issues/20080108093144/20080108100246/MTT8_3_Shotsmans.pdf.

Schreurs, P.J.G., van de Willege, G., Brosschot, J.F., Tellegen, B. and Graus, G.M.H. (1993) *De Utrechtse Coping Lijst: UCL Omgaan met problemen en gebeurtenissen [The Utrecht Coping List: UCL Dealing with Problems and Events]*. Lisse: Swets and Zeitlinger b.v.

Scovel, M.A. and Gardstrom, S.C. (2002) 'Music Therapy within the Context of Psychotherapeutic Models.' In R.F. Unkefer and M.H. Thaut (eds) *Music Therapy in the Treatment of Adults with Mental Disorders: Theoretical Bases and Clinical Interventions*, 2nd edition, 117–132. St Louis, MO: MMB Music.

Shapiro, H. (2003) *Waiting for the man – The Story of Drugs and Popular Music.* London: Helter Skelter Publishing.

Siegel, D. (1999) *The Developing Mind.* New York: Guilford Press.

Silverman, M.J. (2003) 'Music therapy and clients who are chemically dependent: A review of literature and pilot study.' *The Arts in Psychotherapy 30,* 5,273–281.

Silverman, M.J. (2009) 'A descriptive analysis of music therapists working with consumers in substance abuse rehabilitation: Current clinical practice to guide future research.' *The Arts in Psychotherapy 36,* 3, 123–130.

Skaggs, R. (1997) *Finishing Strong: Treating Chemical Addiction with Music and Imagery.* St Louis, MO: MMB Music.

Skewes, K. (2001) *The Experience of Group Music Therapy for Six Bereaved Adolescents.* Unpublished Doctoral Dissertation, University of Melbourne, Australia.

Skille, O. (1989) 'Vibroacoustic Research'. In R. Spintge and R. Droh (eds) *Journal of Music Therapy, 8,* 1, 61–77.

Skille, O. (1991) *Vibroacoustic Therapy: Manual and Reports.* Levanger, Norway: ISVA Publications.

Skille, O. (1992) 'Vibroacoustic Research 1980–1991.' In R. Spintge and R. Droh (eds) *Music Medicine,* 249–266. St Louis, MO: Magna Music Baton.

Skille, O. and Wigram, T. (1995) 'Vibroacoustic Therapy.' In T. Wigram, B. Saperston and R. West (eds) *The Art and Science of Music Therapy: A Handbook,* 23–57. Amsterdam: Harwood Academic Publishers.

Slater, M., Rouner, D., Murphy, K., Beauvais, F., Van Leuven, J. and Domenech-Rodriguez, M. (1996) 'Adolescent counterarguing of TV beer advertisements: Evidence for effectiveness of alcohol education and critical viewing discussions.' *Journal of Drug Education 26,* 2, 143–158.

Small, D.M., Zatorre, R.J., Dagher, A., Evans, A.C. and Jones-Gotman, M. (2001) 'Changes in brain activity related to eating chocolate: From pleasure to aversion.' *Brain 124,* Pt 9, 1720–1733.

Smeijsters, H. (1993) 'Music therapy and psychotherapy.' *The Arts in Psychotherapy 20,* 3, 223–229.

Smeijsters, H. (2005) *Sounding the Self: Analogy in Improvisational Music Therapy.* Gilsum, NH: Barcelona Publishers.

Smith, B. and Smith, D.W. (1995) *The Cambridge Companion to Husserl.* New York: Cambridge University Press.

Soshensky, R. (2001) 'Music therapy and addiction.' *Music Therapy Perspectives 19,* 1, 45–52.

Spitz, H.I. (2001) 'Group therapy of substance abuse in the era of managed mental health care.' *International Journal of Group Psychotherapy 51,* 1, 21–41.

Stefano, G.B., Zhu, W., Cadet, P., Salamon, E. and Mantione, K.J. (2004) 'Music alters constitutively expressed opiate and cytokine processes in listeners.' *Medical Science Monitor 10,* 6, 18–27.

Stern, D.N. (2004) *The Present Moment in Psychotherapy and Everyday Life.* New York: W.W. Norton.

Stevens, J.O. (1971) *Awareness: Exploring, Experimenting, Experiencing.* Moab, UT: Real People Press.

Stoil, M.J. and Blaszczynski, A. (1994) 'Gambling addiction: The nation's dirty little secret.' *Behavioural Health Management 14,* 4, 35–38.

Sugarman, A. and Jaffe, L.S. (1987) 'Transitional Phenomena and Psychological Separateness in Schizophrenic, Borderline and Bulimic Patients.' In J. Bloom-Feshbach and S. Bloom-Feshbach (eds) *The Psychology of Separation and Loss,* 416–456. San Francisco: Jossey-Bass Publishers.

Szasz, T.S. (2003) *Ceremonial Chemistry: The Ritual Persecution of Drugs, Addicts, and Pushers.* Syracuse, New York: Syracuse University Press.

Taeger, H.H. (1988) *Spiritualität und Drogen – Interpersonelle Zusammenhänge von Psychedelika und religiös-mystischen Aspekten in der Gegenkultur der 70er Jahre.* [Spirituality and Drugs–Interpersonal Relationships of Psychedelics and Religious-mystical aspects of 70' counterculture] Markt Erlbach: Raymond Martin.

Tagg, P. (1987) 'Musicology and the semiotics of popular music.' *Semiotica 66,* 1–3, 279–298.

TenBerge, J. (1999) 'Breakdown or breakthrough? A history of European research into drugs and creativity.' *Journal of Creative Behavior 33,* 4, 257–276.

Thaut, M.H. and de l'Etoile, S.K. (1993) 'The effects of music on mood – state-dependent recall.' *Journal of Music Therapy 30,* 2, 70–80.

Thaut, M.H., Nickel, A.K. and Hömberg, V. (2004) 'Neurologische Musiktherapie – Übersicht zum wissenschaftlichen Hintergrund und zur klinischen Methodik' ['Neurologic music therapy: Compendium of scientific background and clinical methodology']. *Musiktherapeutische Umschau 25,* 1, 35–44.

Trapp, E. (2005) 'The push and pull of Hip-Hop: A social movement analysis.' *American Behavioral Scientist 48,* 1482–1495.

Treder-Wolff, J. (1990a) 'Affecting attitudes: Music therapy in addictions treatment.' *Music Therapy Perspectives 8,* 67–71.

Treder-Wolff, J. (1990b) 'Music therapy as a facilitator of creative process in addictions treatment.' *The Arts in Psychotherapy 17,* 4, 319–324.

Treece, C. and Khantzian, E. (1986) 'Psychodynamic factors in the development of drug dependence.' *Psychiatric Clinics of North America 9,* 3, 209–232.

Van Duerzen, E. (1998) *Paradox and Passion in Psychotherapy: An Existential Approach to Psychotherapy and Counselling.* Chichester, Wiley.

van Gennep, A. (1986) *Übergangsriten [Rites of Passage].* Frankfurt: Campus.

Verheul, R. (1997) *The Role of Diagnosing Personality Disorders in Substance Abuse Treatment: Prevalence, Diagnostic Validity and Clinical Implications.* Amsterdam: University Press.

Verheul, R., van den Bosch, L. and Ball, S.A. (2005) 'Substance Abuse.' In J.M. Oldham, A.E. Skodol and D.S. Bender (eds) *The American Psychiatric Publishing Textbook of Personality Disorders,* 463–476. Arlington, VA: American Psychiatric Publishing.

Verres, R. (2007) 'Of angels and other spiritual powers – Orientation in peak experiences' [Electronic Version]. *Music Therapy Today VIII,* 2, 236–256. Retrieved 19 July 2007 from www.musictherapyworld.net/modules/mmmagazine/issues/20070718101131/20070718102011/MTT8_2_Verres.pdf.

Vos, H.P.J. (1989) 'Denial of the inner reality: Observations on drug abuse and addiction based on psychotherapies after treatment in a therapeutic community in the Netherlands.' *Journal of Substance Abuse Treatment 6,* 3, 193–199.

Ward, K.L. (1996) *The Effects of Music Therapy with Chemically Dependent Offenders in a Women's Prison.* Unpublished Master's Thesis. Tallahassee: Florida State University.

Wasson, R.G., Hofmann, A. and Ruck, C.A.P. (1978) *The Road to Eleusis: Unveiling the Secret of the Mysteries.* New York: Harcourt, Brace, Jovanovich.

Watson, D., Clark, L.A. and Tellegen, A. (1988) 'Development and validation of brief measures of positive and negative affect: The PANAS scales.' *Journal of Personality and Social Psychology 54,* 6, 1063–1070.

Weber, K. (1974) 'Veränderungen des Musikerlebens in der experimentellen Psychose (Psylocibin) und ihre Bedeutung für die Musikpsychologie' ['Changes in Music Experience in Experimental Psychosis (psilocybin) and Its Meaning for Music Psychology']. In W.J. Revers, G. Harrer and W.C.M. Simon (eds) *Neue Wege der Musiktherapie [New ways of Music Therapy].* 201–225. Düsseldorf, Wien: Econ Verlag.

Weil, A. (1998) *The Natural Mind.* Boston: Houghton Mifflin.

Weinberg, D. (2002) 'On the embodiment of addiction.' *Body & Society 8,* 4, 1–19.

Wheeler, B. (1981) 'The relationship between music therapy and theories of psychotherapy.' *Music Therapy 1,* 1, 9–16.

Wheeler, B. (1985) 'The relationship between musical and activity elements of music therapy sessions and client responses: An exploratory study.' *Music Therapy 5,* 1, 52–60.

White, W. (1996) *Pathways from the Culture of Addiction to the Culture of Recovery.* Center City, MN: Hazelden Publishers.

Whiteley, S. (1997) 'Altered Sounds.' In A. Melechi (ed.) *Psychedelia Britannica,* 120–142. London: Turnaround.

Whitfield, C. (1989) *Healing the Child Within: Discovery and Recovery for Adult Children of Dysfunctional Families.* Deerfield Beach, FL: Health Communications.

Wigram, T. (1996) *The Effect of Vibroacoustic Therapy on Clinical and Non-Clinical Populations.* Unpublished Doctoral Thesis (PhD), St Georges Hospital Medical School, University of London.

Wigram, T., Nygaard-Pedersen, I. and Bonde, L.O. (2002) *A Comprehensive Guide to Music Therapy: Theory, Clinical Practice, Research and Training.* London: Jessica Kingsley Publishers.

Wilsnack, S.C., Vogeltanz, N.D., Klassen, A.D. and Harris, T.R. (1997) 'Childhood sexual abuse and women's substance abuse: National survey findings.' *Journal of Studies on Alcohol 58,* 3, 264–271.

Winkelman, M. (2003) 'Complementary therapy for addiction: Drumming out drugs.' *American Journal of Public Health 93,* 4, 647–651.

Winnicott, D. (1984) 'Transitional Objects and Transitional Phenomena.' In D. Winnicott *Collected Papers: Through Paediatrics to Psychoanalysis,* 229–242. London: H. Karnac Books Ltd. (Original work published 1951.)

Winnicott, D.W. (1965) *The Maturational Process and the Facilitating Environment: Studies in the Theory of Emotional Development.* London: Hogarth Press.

Wurmser, L. (1985) 'Denial and split identity: Timely issues in the psychoanalytic treatment of compulsive drug users.' *Journal of Substance Abuse Treatment 2,* 2, 89–96.

Yacubian, J. and Büchel, C. (2009) 'The Genetic Basis of Individual Differences in Reward Processing and the Link to Addictive Behavior.' In J.C. Dreher and L. Tremblay (eds) *Handbook of Reward and Decision Making,* 345–360. Burlington: Academic Press.

Yalom, I.D. (1995) *The Theory and Practice of Group Psychotherapy,* [Rezepive Musiktherapie im Strafvollzug] 4th edition. New York: Basic Books.

Zeuch, A. (2001) 'Receptive music therapy in penality.' *Zeitschrift fuer Musik-, Tanz und Kunsttherapie 12,* 1, 13–20.

Subject Index

Author Index